DANCING TO A
DIFFERENT TUNE

Patrick L. Schmidt

DANCING TO A DIFFERENT TUNE

Interviews, essays and commentaries
on the intercultural experience

MERIDIAN WORLD PRESS   SIETAREUROPA

CANADIAN CATALOGING IN PUBLISHING DATA

Schmidt, Patrick L., 1949 –

Dancing to a different tune — Interviews, essays and commentaries on the intercultural experience.

ISBN 978-0-9685293-4-8

1. Intercultural studies — Cross-cultural studies,
2. Intercultural communication — Cross-cultural communication

GRAPHIC DESIGN & TYPESETTING
Axel Wendelberger

Printed in the United Kingdom.

MERIDIAN WORLD PRESS
8, rue Daniel Hirtz
67000 Strasbourg, France
Phone: +33 3 884 436 52
Email: patrick.schmidt49@gmail.com

MERIDIAN WORLD PRESS   SIETAREUROPA

ACKNOWLEDGMENTS

As with many intellectual endeavors, this book is the result of a particular history as well as a series of unrelated events. Nearly six years ago, the SIETAR Europa Board realized a newsletter was needed to keep members up to date with the latest intercultural news. I volunteered to take up the task, thinking it would involve a modest amount of work. A few issues later, the newsletter had evolved into a magazine and I was putting in many more hours than expected, doing interviews, articles and reviews in addition to editing those of contributors. It was, however, due to the continual support and cooperation of SIETAR Europa that I was able to fulfill this mission to the full extent of my passion. I wish to recognize and thank the Board here.

Others to whom I am indebted are, of course, the interviewees who generously shared their stories. These are people from all walks of life whose frank, often perceptive observations—on intercultural communication, cultural integration and the challenges of mutual understanding and accommodation—have made our profession more dynamic and given it a wider audience.

I would also like to sincerely thank Axel Wendelberger, my graphic designer, whose vision of what an intercultural book should look like was the initial force that led me to make it a reality. Only through his tenacious encouragement was the project realized. Also to Jenny Flechsenhar, who took great care in reading the final version, making astute editorial points. And Dan MacLeod, my dear copy editor. For almost two decades, he has been my indispensable ally and friend. No writer could ever have had a more diligent, intelligent and hard-hitting editor. His severe truths about what good writing is still echo in my mind and I shudder to think what would have been printed had he not been there.

And lastly my wife Jacqueline. Without her support, patience and enduring love, this book would have remained but a dream.

Contents

EXAMINING THE DANCE

BOOK REVIEWS AND COMMENTARIES

Introduction

This book is neither a compendium of "dos and don'ts" nor yet another ode to cross-cultural perspectives. It is a record of the personal journeys of the founders and builders of interculturalism as a concept, then as a new field of social science. How and why they became who they are and what they now represent. What they feel—looking back as well as forward—about the birth of interculturalism, its evolution thus far, its future. What they teach and how they live it today.

Just as the present book is the story of people's journeys from all corners of the planet to the intercultural world, it is also mine.

When I was 10 years old, my parents thought it would be good for me to see life beyond suburban Los Angeles so they sent me to spend the summer with my grandparents, who lived in a small village in Alsace, France. The vacation stretched into 15 months, I attended the local village school, French became my dominant language and I became far less American.

By the time I got back to California, my perception of the world had radically changed. I found myself dancing back and forth between French and American subjective worlds, not really knowing where I belonged. My sojourn in France had, in some ways, triggered an unbearable sense of floating, almost of non-identity.

Ironically, the experience gave me the wanderlust to spend my life discovering other cultural realities. After college, I went back to Europe and, for some reason of fate, ended up living in Stuttgart. I would spend the next 20 years immersed in the German way of being, becoming German myself in many ways.

I also began to realize—teaching English to Germans while I learned German myself—that understanding and generating appropriate behavior is an integral part of language training. Without knowing it, I was becoming an interculturalist.

The map of my life would come to include years in Malaysia, in French Canada, then Austria. I went from teaching English to editing business magazines to establishing cross-cultural programs, corporate workshops and university courses in…interculturalism. My *modus vivendi* became my career.

As with many people, I discovered SIETAR (*Society of Intercultural Education, Training and Research*) just about the time I found myself looking more closely at our field. Later, I had the opportunity to serve on the SIETAR Europa Board as secretary, then treasurer and finally president, coming into contact and sharing experiences with some extraordinary, and eternally curious, people. By now I realized interculturalism wasn't just a skill-set, it was my life.

The book is based on a simple idea from my college days in southern California, that the best way to understand something is to write about it. Two decades later, it was what guided me to reflect on my years in the German business world, resulting in *Understanding American and German Business Cultures*.

Putting my insights and perceptions down on paper made me more aware of my own cultural conditioning and of assumptions and values which lie outside my awareness. Writing it was no picnic but the reward—a true understanding of American-German relations—was worth the struggle. Europeans would call this an inductive form of learning and it is very American indeed: pro-active, simplistic, *learn-by-doing*.

That same idea was the spark that led to launching the SIETAR *Europa Journal*, which I've had the privilege of developing over the past six years. My vision from the beginning has been to feature the viewpoints and unique experiences of those at the forefront of the intercultural world, while enhancing the SIETAR name—and the field itself—with a solid magazine.

I have always made it a point in my interviews to ask about the interviewee's early life, a gentle way of entering into another person's psyche. Learning about childhood experiences and how they marked an individual's personality is always fascinating and it gives distinct clues as to why that person later chose the intercultural field. After a good interview, I walk away feeling I've had a glimpse of a personal universe of thought, a certain understanding, something shared.

Dancing to a Different Tune is a collection of interviews, articles and critiques that I've written for the *Journal*. It sums up a lifetime of trying to reach beyond the cultural and linguistic boundaries that limit us. The pieces are designed to demystify the intercultural process, impart objectivity and sensitivity, inform our perceptions of globalization, of business in general, even provide a new look at history.

The first section deals essentially with the lives of people who have consciously engaged themselves in developing their intercultural sensitivity. The second looks at the ways subjective minds can be aligned with the currents of globalization and international commerce. The third examines how the intercultural theme can be applied to a variety of areas, ranging from history, linguistics and education to personal experiences. The final section is a review of some of the many excellent books (and a film) that reflect the huge interest in this field.

A word about my articles: they have a strong tilt toward German, Austrian and American cultures, which reflects the many years of living in those countries. Nonetheless, the lessons and principles found in these writings are meant to be extrapolated, applicable to all cultures.

Assembling the myriad themes is to underline the cardinal rule of our profession, that the acquisition of intercultural skills is not an end in itself. Rather, it is to widen personal horizons and generate alternative experiences—the rhythmic intuition of cross-cultural dance.

Becoming sensitive to *feelings of appropriateness,* the "inherent logic" of diverse human behavior, enriches us with a new cultural universe. To instinctively capture unknown, untested reality in its proper context is an intense adventure, which resonates deeply, organically. A sensitivity that is becoming more and more necessary in our wonderfully diverse, often mysterious world. If this book can clarify that process, I will have achieved my goal.

DANCING THE TUNE OF
INTERCULTURAL SENSITIVITY

Interview with Milton Bennett

Developing intercultural sensitivity

The development of intercultural sensitivity has taken on an importance that no one could have imagined 15 or 20 years ago. Due to the ever-increasing influence of globalization, the internet and even Twitter, cross-cultural contact has become almost a daily occurrence. The different languages, behavior patterns and values enrich our lives but also leave us confused and lead to cultural faux pas. Our job is to understand why, then develop new skills to communicate and behave appropriately in different settings.

Milton Bennett's *Developmental Model of Intercultural Sensitivity,* more commonly known as the DMIS, is a remarkable explanation of what the mind does when confronting intercultural difference. It's a powerful theoretical framework, incorporating notions of empathy, consciousness and subjective relativity that shed light on the cognitive functioning of the brain. Each stage indicates a particular perceptional mode and behavior. By recognizing the underlying orientation toward culture difference, you can make predictions about people's behavior; training can be tailored to facilitate development into following stages. It's an intriguing, yet simple, description of what human beings do in new cultural surroundings.

Even more interesting is the road Dr. Bennett took in arriving at his conclusions. Everything began with his desire to understand "the act of creation" as a young, 20-year old student at Stanford University. Twenty-two years and countless experiences later, his tenacious curiosity led to the publication of this intercultural benchmark. I had the opportunity to talk to him in Milan and learn about his extraordinary intellectual journey.

Let's start with your early life-experiences…

Soon after I was born in Boston, my parents moved to Seattle, where I spent my first eight years. After that we lived a couple of years in Stockton, California. All I can remember about Stockton was that it was flat and I was able to ride my bicycle. From the age of ten, I lived in a small town outside Portland, Oregon. The schools in McMinnville provided a better education than I would have experienced in a big city. And there was a small liberal arts college, which had a large number of foreign students.

So more diversity than a normal small town?

Yes, but I was used to differences. When we lived in Seattle, my mother used to take me to other places in the city that were not so homogenous as where we lived, just to give me the experience of being around people who were different.

Another thing my parents did was host a student sponsored by AFS (American Field Service). He came from Hamburg, Germany, and became a good friend. After graduating from high school, I did a three-month tour of Europe with Helmut, who really perked my interest in other cultures.

Also my father became the international marketing representative at the small company he worked for. He ended up travelling a lot to Europe and Asia and made me acutely aware of the importance of international business.

Obviously, your curiosity about cultural differences came to you early in life. Did you want to become an interculturalist from the beginning?

No, not at all. Through high school, I had two big interests—one was science and the other was writing. I participated in national science projects, was given scholarships and sent off to science camps. My studies began at Stanford University, where I majored in physics for a couple of years but realized I didn't really want to do that. I found myself moving to the other side of my interests and joined the creative writing program at Stanford.

Interesting things were happening in the mid-60s. I got involved in research at the Palo Alto Medical Center, taking part in early experiments with LSD. At that time LSD was legal and seen as a consciousness exploration; it was taken seriously by researchers. There were a lot of safeguards and always someone there who could intercede if anything went wrong. I had some interesting experiences and wrote about them in psychology classes. What LSD does is to lower interconceptual boundaries, so there's a flowing of one thing into another. Some of the insights in my work were facilitated by those "trips".

I ended up graduating with a creative writing degree and the upshot of that was I became interested in cognitive psychology—how the mind creates. "The act of creation", to borrow the phrase from Arthur Koestler's book; writers are tuned in to that. The combination of LSD-exploration and cognitive psychology came together to provide me with motivation to explain this interesting act of consciousness. How does it work? Why would it work that way?

I decided to do a masters degree in psycho-linguistics at San Francisco State University. I thought this would be interesting to explore the psychology of language as a way of understanding the act of creation and consciousness in general. It was a combination of general semantics, more or less based on linguistic relativity; the *Whorf/Sapir Hy-*

The Act of Creation was published in 1964 and influenced Milton Bennett's view on creativity.

pothesis was central to this movement. The basic idea of general semantics—which has been largely lost—is that many problems in the way we think about things have to do with the "reification" of language.*

Misapprehensions are related to that. For instance, some say the most dangerous word in the English language is "is", because it's taken as a statement of reality rather than as a linguistic convention to create a representation of something.

So you wanted to know how linguistics, in the context of creative writing, affects our representation of ourselves and others...

You could say so. And I shifted to the meta level, seeing myself as somebody interested in explaining things, being creative in the explanation of description rather than a generator of artistic creativity. I did the course-work, which was very interesting, then joined the Peace Corps and was assigned to Micronesia.

What was the Peace Corps like at that time?

The Peace Corps was in transition, moving from pre-departure to on-site training. The pre-departure consisted of exposing us to a set of grueling psychological stress tests. The

---

    *   The fallacy of treating an abstraction as if it were a real thing.

idea was if the local inhabitants attacked you psychologically and you could resist, that would make you a good volunteer.

Then they dropped us on an island called Truk, now called Chuuk. They left us alone except for language classes; it was a sort of sink-or-swim immersion. The program was run by former volunteers who had no sophistication in talking about the culture—

In the early 1970s Milton Bennett taught children in Micronesia.

nothing about communication, values, beliefs or behavior. There was a little bit about etiquette, but only as a side-effect of the language.

The only thing good was the language-training; classes were excellent and we lived with a family who didn't speak any English. This generated, in my mind, the idea of being a "fluent fool": you know the language but nothing about the culture. In 1998 I published *How Not to Be a Fluent Fool* and discovered that Winston Bremback had already coined the term.

Those two years in the Peace Corps were both mind-blowing and mind-numbing. There were moments of complete boredom and, at times, tremendous change. Looking back, my major experience was learning and speaking Trukese to the point of being negotiable at some of the most complex levels of that society.

What did you do after your time with the Peace Corps?

I came back to finish writing my master's thesis. It was about empathy and sympathy. I think empathy describes the mechanism of consciousness-shifting. Empathy is intentionally setting up the condition of trying to apprehend another's experience sufficiently to feel "as if" you are having that experience yourself. This is the basis of all good communication, although people mostly think of it as a therapy technique. Empathy is particularly necessary for intercultural communication.

I was really interested in intentional consciousness-shifting, whether facilitated by LSD, done through meditation, or a basic act of creation such as a novelist might engage in. I believe it's an extension of boundaries, allowing yourself to move through something that's not your normal experience. The same could be said about an artistic happening, such as watching a ballet or appreciating a sculpture, you're "taken in" by aesthetic empathy.

At the same time, I was doing some interesting studies on voluntary control of internal states: bio-feedback and certain paranormal phenomena like remote-viewing, where one's perception seems to be located outside or even at a distance from one's body.

Upon finishing your thesis, you continued your studies on extending boundaries?

Yes, but I wasn't sure how to go about it. Then I got a call from Dean Barnlund, a former professor who was organizing a conference at the International Christian University at Mitaka, outside Tokyo. I said to myself, "If he thinks I should go, I'm going!" I had no money but I went out and borrowed it. As it turned out, it was a seminal conference in intercultural communication. It was in 1972 and a lot of the early intercultural people were there and many decisions were made, one being to set up SIETAR.

Then a second fateful thing happened. Our Japanese guide got drunk at dinner and the train he put us on was going in the wrong direction. I was with Bill Howell, who was setting up a doctoral program in Intercultural Communications. At the end of our long trip he said, "Why don't you come to the University of Minnesota?"

You accepted his invitation?

Yes, to do the program as well as teach intercultural workshops; they date back to the mid-60s in Pittsburgh and were based on Edward Hall's work targeting foreign students. Now they were being used for all kinds of students, not just foreign, to explore ethnic differences, what we call diversity today.

Did the workshops deepen your knowledge of consciousness-shifting?

Yes. But intercultural communication is not unique in supposing there's some kind of "shift" necessary to appreciate someone else's experience. In certain types of therapy the level of intensity demands a bigger act of empathy on the part of the therapist than does everyday communication. The same thing happens at artistic events. And leadership is also related to context-shifting. People at the Harvard Leadership Initiative call it "contextual intelligence", the ability to be aware of context and to shift. Intercultural communication is an operationalization of shifting consciousness.

Another powerful thing about the program at Minnesota was the dissertation work I did on the "forming-feeling process", an early attempt to say perception is really about apprehending the feeling of something and communication is about giving form to that. Antonio Demasio wrote a book on this, *The Feeling of What Happens*. The forming is more the categorization, the structuring of the experience. I called this a system of "processual complementarity", meaning that these two sides were constantly being reconciled—it's a dialectic that maintains itself.

What you're saying is that intercultural competence is a more sophisticated description of the feeling?

There are two levels here, Patrick. One is of someone moving through that sequence, acquiring a more sophisticated experience of cultural difference by having more sophisticated strategies for describing, giving form to the experience.*

[When the employee came] we first reacted angrily and said to ourselves, "He's an idiot!" Then we have our cultural informant describe the context, in that hotels in Italy are now required by law to check everyone going to a room for reasons of terrorism. This is organizing that experience in a more sophisticated way. So rather than say something simplistic—"He's an idiot!"—we say, "Well this is an interesting situation." We don't necessarily prefer it but we see how this fits in to a more general cultural pattern of some sort.

The same thinking often happens at the end of my workshops. Participants say, "If we'd known this before, we'd have avoided misunderstandings with our foreign colleagues. Now we have a more coherent structure."

Yes, what you're doing is taking them through that process, giving them a more sophisticated way of understanding. In a lot of cases, it's retroactive: they'll reflect on the experience they had and say, "Now, I see what was happening."

The other thing is on the meta level; the DMIS itself is a description of how people get better at this. All of us, carry around certain trailing tendencies and one of them is a little bit of superiority and familiarity with our own culture and a little bit of a negative response when something happens that's different. The question is how quickly can we reconstrue the experience with more sophisticated categories?

---

* This interview took place in my hotel room but, before we could get started, we were told Dr. Bennett had to return downstairs and register. Ironically, this annoyance provided us an excellent example of "forming-feeling".

You mean to have a more neutral, appropriate view?

Yes. Here our cultural informant says the employee was a little overzealous but not really an idiot, which allows us to reframe. How open are we? Assuming we're further along the developmental sequence, we're looking for resolutions. We're distrustful of our gut reaction if we think it may be ethnocentric. When he told us to register, we initially reacted in an ethnocentric manner, not as an Italian would.

However, we have to be careful in not accepting everything as cultural. In some situations the other person is an idiot [and] acting wrongly in his or her cultural context. If we're unable to see how that person is acting inappropriately, we're being just as insensitive as if we were ethnocentric.

To get back to my PhD work, it was the theoretical extension of the master's program, consciousness-shifting, but going into the more general theory of how perception and communication were operating in this forming-feeling process. This established the theoretical base for being able to talk about consciousness-shifting in general. I began teaching courses on consciousness and paranormal communication and did this for a number of years but I slowly began doing more and more intercultural work. I've never seem them being as distinct.

So you could say intercultural communication is a form of paranormal communication?

Yes, it's paranormal in the sense that it's not what we normally do. But it's in the realm of human capabilities.

How, then, did the DMIS come into being?

It was a combination of those two things, running intercultural workshops and doing consciousness studies. All the time my brain is organizing stuff around forming, feeling, extension, empathy—all this consciousness work I'm doing.

The original motivation for the DMIS was training methodology. In the mid-'80s, methods were often thrown together in haphazard ways. A lot of concern was for pacing issues, like you should do simulation after lunch because it keeps people awake. There was no pedagogical sequencing or logical consideration. I wanted to answer the questions "How can we sequence this material better in training programs?" [and] "What do we hope people will be able to do at the end of this?"

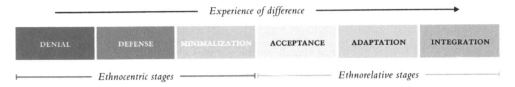

The different stages of Bennett's *Developmental Model of Intercultural Sensitivity* (DMIS)

This was an early attempt to define intercultural competence. I'd define the end-state as integration—the ability to shift from one state to another—whether it be bicultural or multicultural—what I now call an expanded repertoire of worldview.

What's the beginning state? Some of my early studies at Portland were around cults: a little model of an ethnocentric culture, very strong. People who otherwise might not be ethnocentric join these groups and become ethnocentric. Those who run the Moonies and, to some extent, the Scientologists really know which buttons to push. The caution is to recognize the process, not the nonsense being said. I defined the process cult-leaders use in generating followings and, to my surprise, it was later published in a book for FBI agents!

When it came time to define what is ethnocentric, I had a pretty good idea: the experience of your own culture as central to your reality. All of us are, to some extent, convinced about our set of beliefs… religious, national, etcetera. The cult-people think their view of reality is completely and uniquely central to reality.

So what is the beginning state? It's this experience of your own culture as being central and it moves through this forming-feeling process that I name stages—they're really more positions along the continuum than stages. What you're doing is marking different organizations of experience; the DMIS is based on subjective organization. The more complex structure you have for dealing with cultural differences, the deeper the experience you have.

How does this different organization of experience actually work?

There are two levels. My ability to understand you depends on my having a relatively complex facsimile of you and your experience. That said, I also need to have a relatively complex explanation for how it is that I go about apprehending that experience. So not only do I need to have the idea that you're a complex human being, but I also have to have an infrastructure that allows me to take that perspective. And both of those things are developing simultaneously in the DMIS.

In the ethnocentric condition, I have virtually no sense of the complexity of the other. I have this complete simplification of anything outside of my own experience [but] I may have a pretty complex experience of my own context.

To go back to the point, the movement through the developmental model is [that of] forming feelings, getting better at consciousness-shifting. I think that the DMIS represented a formalization, in an intercultural context, of all the work I'd been doing on consciousness from my last two years at Stanford up 'til 1986. In those 22 years, it had all come together.

So the DMIS came out of creative writing, LSD experiments, linguistics, the Peace Corps, foreign students, and paranormal and intercultural studies. There wasn't a conscious effort to say "I'm going to discover the stages people go through when adapting to other cultures."

You could say that. The impetus to write the DMIS came from workshops which asked "What do we do next?" I articulated this in Michael Paige's book *Cross-Cultural Orientation* or in a special issue of *IJIR* (International Journal of Intercultural Relations), I forget which... Both occurred pretty much at the same time in 1986 [and] the response led to the re-publication of the DMIS in a somewhat more sophisticated form in 1993. Since then, I've been refining it. It was about 2004 when I did my last major rewrite and I'll probably do another one soon.

Turning to another subject. In your opinion, what are the important issues today in the intercultural field?

One is the increasing diffusion of our conceptual boundaries. For various reasons it's becoming less clear who we are, not more clear. The field of intercultural communication or intercultural relations, whatever you want to call it, is experiencing a kind of diffusion into a variety of other disciplines, such as sociology, anthropology, etcetera.

There are fewer and fewer programs at universities dedicated to intercultural communication and more and more an inclusion of an intercultural dimension to other programs. The effect is that the underlying assumptive base of the field is unclear; it tends to take on the base of whatever the discipline is, so the MBA takes on MBA assumptions and cross-cultural psychology takes on psychology assumptions.

And the original synthesis of anthropology, language and communication is, I would say, becoming more unclear. I'd like to compensate for that by clarifying those boundaries and I think we could do this by sponsoring meetings, incorporating the conversation into our SIETAR meetings and making sure it gets included in interviews like this one.

How does all this fit into the virtual world?

Like any educational enterprise, which interculturalism is, we need to deal with the fact that education is operating increasingly in a virtual environment. People expect virtual treatment of things and operations, such as multicultural teams, so the virtuality of those situations needs to be addressed in what we do. However, if we don't come to that conversation about extension into the virtual with a clear set of assumptions about who we are, and who we are not, then it will be nothing but an exercise in pop futurology.

I notice this among companies. They want to make virtual teams more effective in no time flat but they don't want to spend time and resources in a kick-off meeting, where the teams are physically together for three days.

Right, and if we in the field of interculturalism aren't clear about what we do and what we don't do, about who we are and who we aren't, we can't come into those kinds of situations with a clear vision of how to do this. We become effective by saying, "Here's what you have to do and here's what you don't need to do."

And this raises a second issue: Techniques have overwhelmed theory. In our field there's been a faster growth of methodology—of technique, including measurements—than in the underlying theory of what we're doing and why we're doing it.

We interculturalists have spent a lot of time generating techniques, methods, procedures, implementation-strategies, applications. And we've spent relatively less time—in fact there may have been an active disinterest on the part of many people—on what the underlying conceptual structure is. Another way of saying it is that we're reifying the techniques. We're treating the techniques as the thing we're teaching, rather than using techniques as a way to get people to attain understanding of something. The means have come to be substituted for the ends in many cases.

This is largely because people without much preparation are attempting to conduct intercultural education and training. They take one TOT (training of trainer) course and say, "Hey, this is a rather cool thing! Lots of fun and you can charge for it, too!" But they really don't know what the history of the field is or what the theoretical grounds are.

I don't know if our field is more susceptible to people like that. I suspect maybe it is, because interculturalists tend to confuse ethnorelativism with being non-judgmental. So they refrain from making judgments such as the one I just stated for fear that they are being bigoted or prejudicial. They engage in non-critical acceptance not just of cultural differences, but of every idea and practice. Yet intercultural sensitivity doesn't mean being non-judgmental, it means making judgments in a culturally-appropriate way. In the case of a field of study and practice such as intercultural communication, it is not only appropriate, but crucial to make judgments about one's own and others' professional competence.

What would you recommend to young people who want to get into a graduate program of interculturalism?

The general advice to someone who's going to do graduate work is: Pay attention to who, not where. Rather than deciding you're going to go to Oxford, say "Who is it at Oxford that I have something to learn from and what makes me think so?"

Good programs exist but are separated in different departments, which might be education, anthropology, psychology, linguistics. For instance, I can speak of an intercultural program I know, the University of Milano-Bicocca. It's in a sociology department—not a communication or anthropology department—and is associated with programs in social work and international cooperation. But it's a very sophisticated intercultural program.

That's the kind of thing someone needs to look into: Who's associated with the program and what's the depth of the intercultural dimension of that program? People who ask that question need to know the difference between cultural and intercultural because there are lots of programs out there that are essentially cultural. Or, even further removed, there're political, like so-called "intercultural dialogue programs".

Such programs are almost always attempting to reduce international or interethnic tensions—prejudice-reduction. That's a good thing, but the programs usually don't address the development of intercultural competence at all. So the term intercultural is being used to mean something like cross-cultural. There are two cultures involved but nothing about the process of creating inter-subjectivity or any of the other communication terms that we'd use.

So the student who's looking for a program needs to have done enough reading to know the difference between an intercultural and a "cultural" program?

Yes, that's right. Secondly, I'd recommend a young person to think about the following: Sophisticated theory generates powerful applications. By sophisticated theory, I mean having a coherent set of assumptions about culture, cultural identity, intercultural relations, and the development of intercultural competence. By powerful applications, I mean using those coherent assuptions to select and implement effective interventions in cross-cultural and multicultural situations.

Unfortunately, the usual case is application without underlying coherent theory—the increasing tendency for intercultural practice to be separated from intercultural theory. While we always claim to be turning theory into practice, the reality is that we are usually elaborating practice with, at best, some theoretical rationalization.

I think the criterion for every technique we have—whether it be role-play, simulation, inventory measurement, or any other kind—should be, "How does this activity fit with other activities being offered in this program to enact a theory of intercultural competence?"

This mentality is something I've incorporated into the programs I've worked with, including the Master's in Intercultural Relations offered through the University of the Pacific and the Intercultural Communication Institute and most recently the IDR Academy sponsored by the Intercultural Development Research Institute.

So my advice to a young person is, "Know what you're looking for. Pay attention to who it is you're studying with, not just where you're studying." And, second, "Sophisticated theory generates powerful applications," so look for the former and the latter will follow.

Well Milton, on behalf of the members of SIETAR Europa, I would like to thank you for this most interesting interview.

My pleasure.

Interview with Vincent Merk

Moving beyond one's culture

Expatriation is a phenomenon that has been with us since the beginning of civilization. In the broad sense, an expatriate is any person living in a foreign land. From the Latin *expatriare*—gone out from one's country—its most common usage today concerns professionals sent abroad by their companies.

Giving up one's native culture to live where one's identity and frames of reference are radically transformed is, literally, mind-blowing. The renowned painting *Wanderer Above the Sea of Fog,* created in 1818 by the German romantic artist Caspar David Friedrich, symbolizes well the expatriate's mind. It's a message of self-reflection, at the same time a metaphor for the unknown.

The whole process of expatriation can be viewed in this manner: contemplating one's unique self while confronting an unknown future in a foreign culture. It's a dialectic conversation—leaving one's culture means generating the will to master a new landscape of behavior and also coming to understand the insignificance of the individual within it.

Someone who has contemplated the intercultural experience and its consequences is Vincent Merk. Raised and educated in Strasbourg, he is a pure product of French culture and Cartesian logic. But if you talk to his students at the Einhoven University of Technology, they'd tell you their professor is Dutch all the way, both in language and thought.

Merk has lived in Holland since 1981. Coordinator of the Language and Communication Centre and senior lecturer in intercultural management at Eindhoven University of Technology, he also works as an intercultural business consultant and has numerous articles and books on the subject. When SIETAR began in Europe, he was one of its first members and served as president from 1997–99.

With a powerful physical presence and a deep, strong voice, he looks like the CEO of an international corporation. But you quickly realize his passion is interculturalism, which has made him a leading expert in French-Dutch communications. Thanks to the challenges he faced in adapting to his new country, he learned the art of weaving in and out of different realities, becoming a dynamic and engaging personality in his field. In this interview, he discusses the intercultural experience and its consequences on relations between people and countries.

Perhaps we can begin by having you tell us about your formative years.

I was born in Strasbourg, a family of five children. My parents were both teachers, which meant we naturally spoke French at home. It was an ambiguous situation because some of my friends spoke the Germanic/Allemanish dialect, Alsatian. My parents used it when they didn't want us children to understand but we were learning German at school so we soon understood some of it.

Many of my friends were dialectophone, Alsatian was their mother tongue. They learned to speak German quickly, not correctly. Those good in Alsatian and German had more trouble with French but I was a bit jealous — as a francophone, I had trouble with German grammar. In a way, I blamed my parents a bit for not speaking Alsatian to us.

The reason was World War II. Alsace was incorporated into the German Reich and it impacted my family immensely. This was not exceptional, in Alsatian intellectual circles children were brought up in French. Alsatian was the language of the working class. It wasn't like Luxembourg, where the bourgeoisie spoke a mixture of French and German. Still, it was a typical bilingual area in which some spoke both languages and others did not.

Did living in that environment give you a more expanded intercultural horizon than that of French people not from Alsace?

Oh yes, I always had this impression of being somewhat more "sophisticated" than the *Français de l'intérieur*. I was living on the border in an international city. I think this is true of people living in any border-city, such as Bolzano in the South Tyrol or Biel in Switzerland.

I felt 100% French but with a special identity. I could certainly be a link, as Alsatians are in general, to the French who lived in another world. That created the basis for my intercultural life later on.

And how did your intercultural life begin?

Until the age of 18, I was just a kid from France who had a family with an open mind, living on the border with Germany and having connections to Germany and other countries. I knew early on that I was going to live somewhere else. I like France but I wanted to study abroad.

After doing my French baccalauréat, I spent a year in a small town in Illinois, between Chicago and St. Louis (AFS Program). This was probably the biggest experience of my youth, being a senior in an American high school and staying with a family of educators.

Everybody wanted to go to the East or West Coast and I ended up in the mid-West. I thought I knew the U.S. from television and magazines but it was very different from what I expected, a kind of a culture shock. And yet, it gave me total immersion into an American family and really opened my mind to other cultures.

Afterward I went back to France to study in Strasbourg and Grenoble, doing a master's in public administration with emphasis on foreign languages — German, English and Dutch. Then I got a one-year scholarship to a post-graduate program in communication at the University of Amsterdam and it went so well they extended my scholarship for another year.

It was normal to return to your home-country to begin your career but I felt comfortable in Holland. I got a job at the university, lecturing and teaching French, but, very quickly, the department had me doing more and more intercultural work, such as international negotiations. That was almost 30 years ago.

Vincent Merk spent the first 18 years of his life in Strasbourg, which at that time was a vibrant bi-lingual city of French and German.

Did the university introduce you to interculturalism?

Not really. I'd become intercultural with my stay in the U.S., my language studies, summer courses in Germany, Belgium and Holland, and living in the Netherlands. It was already my daily life. With some theoretical background, the university allowed me to develop, teach it, research it—interculturalism became my life. Or as the Dutch say, it was a hobby that went out of control!

Let's go on to identity. I found it interesting that people take you for a native speaker. You say you don't mind that people take you for a Dutchman but, if you get into a deeper conversation, you can get irritated if they think you're Dutch. I suppose that in your heart of hearts, you feel very French.

Oh yes. My first 18 years were spent in France, which makes me French. But because I was living on the border I had some openings to the Germanic world. Now that I've lived longer in the Netherlands than in France I have a bit of a split personality, like many expats!

But I feel French and will defend France because I hear so much nonsense about France. I'm the first one to stand up in the Netherlands and say, "This is stupid, this is wrong"; I do the same for the Netherlands in France. In this respect, I'm typically bicultural in that I feel both countries and cultures.

In my Dutch family, I'm French and am very much the typical French father to my daughter. But beyond that, outside the family circle, I'm integrated with Dutch society. My colleagues and friends know I'm French but they can't believe it basically—to them, I'm very much Dutch.

Going on to another area—your Dutch students. Are they more sophisticated in intercultural issues than 25 years ago?

I think there's a double evolution here. On the one hand, they know a lot more about the outside world than my generation, through television, the internet, all the media. And they travel a lot more. They want to go to Australia, South America, South Africa. They often do their graduate thesis abroad and have enormous baggage when they graduate.

At the same time, they're more limited in their views. The Anglo-Saxon world is attractive but France, Italy, Spain—that's too close or too "foreign". When I started lecturing here 25 years ago, students went to those countries in masses.

Now there's a kind of indifference or fear of other European cultures because they don't master the languages anymore. Before the war, Holland had a lot of francophiles and germanophiles. The war came and that was it for German culture. Interest in France survived until the 80s but now it's just Anglo-American language and culture.

So very few students are trilingual. I was originally hired to teach French and taught for about 25 years: "le français pour ingénieur". I stopped four years ago when only three students registered!

Our biggest problem is to get Dutch students to go to German universities — it's not exotic enough, they all want to go to Australia! And they don't speak the language any more so they have this fear and, at the same time, blasé attitude toward Germany. Yet a lot of Germans come to the Netherlands because we have our master's programs in English and the university has a very good reputation.

Dutch people today overwhelmingly speak English, to the detriment of other foreign languages.

How did you get involved in SIETAR *?*

Actually, somebody told me about SIETAR early on and I went to a conference in Denver back in 1988. I was very enthusiastic, I knew it was the association for me: SIETAR gave me the chance to participate in interculturalism at all levels.

Then, in 1990, we had an international conference in Kilkenny, Ireland. A lot of European members went and it triggered the founding of SIETAR Europa (SE). We had our first conference in Haarlem in 1991 and 30 people attended, me being one of them. I contributed by doing some work behind the scenes and became a member of the Board in 1995. I stayed on for four years and was president the last two.

I'm proud to say I've been to all the SE congresses except for one in Italy in 1992. There are two reasons why I enjoy them, the first being the knowledge you gain, you learn about the latest research. Of course, the second is networking with your peers. These yearly gatherings have a re-energizing effect on me.

The last congress I attended was in Berlin a few weeks ago and the main theme was cosmopolitan communication. While reflecting on it, I wonder if we weren't trying to reinvent the wheel. Is cosmopolitan communication not just another term for reconciliation of different values — respect one another and try to make a new culture from it? Basically, it's also dilemma reconciliation.

Trompenaars bases his whole theory on this. I don't want to say he was the first to discover it but his dilemma reconciliation is what interculturalism is all about. It's not either-or, which is Western logic. Rather, you have two opposites and you need to reconcile and find symbiosis.

Talking about symbiosis, you're an expert in French-Dutch relations. What are the biggest differences between the two nations and how do you get the French and Dutch to work together?

Basically you could say these are two cultures with just Belgium in the middle, which is not a coincidence. Culturally speaking, they are rather far from one another. It's the Anglo-Saxon, Calvinist world meets the Latin-Catholic world. Pragmatism versus improvised solutions.

It's also a big country and a small one, as well as north versus south. France is not really south but is certainly at the crossroads of north and south. You see this on a daily basis in communication: Dutch are low-context, you call a cat a cat. Contrast this to the more high-context French—indirect, abstract, more formal. The "vous" is still prevalent in France, whereas, in Holland, "u" (formal you) is less and less used.

To arrive at cooperation, my approach is the four "Rs" of Trompenaars. First thing is to create recognition. Very often they don't know about one another's values and practices. The Dutch have been to summer camping sites in France, and the French think the Netherlands is a cross between Scandinavia and Germany. Conflicts happen because they don't know one another.

After attaining recognition, you can generate respect, and possibly also acceptance and appreciation. Once you've done that, you strive to reconcile differences and find best-practices. You see issues in their reality: what are the problems? You root this new knowledge to practices, some sort of procedure.

All great leaders see differences and try to reconcile them. Edgar Schein once said "culture is the way a group of people solves problems and reconciles dilemmas." I think that makes a lot of sense. When everything goes well you don't feel culture, only when faced with problems. When something's at stake, you feel culture. And there is always a way to solve a dilemma.

Interview with Vinita Balasubramanian

The Indian mindset

Mindsets play an important role in maintaining social cohesion. Defined as a set of assumptions about reality, they reflect a group's history and underlying philosophical leitmotivs, as well as the external spheres of influence which may have impacted its development. The group viewpoint is so well engrained that people are often not consciously aware of how it shapes decision-making and behavioral interaction.

Upon studying the Indian mindset, observers will immediately note that Hinduism has profoundly influenced the country. It's a philosophy that doesn't try to be a religion in the classic sense — it makes no claim on any one Prophet and teaches openness and universal tolerance of differences. This helps explain why India is so multicultural, given that the Hindu way of thinking permits an assimilation of cultures, languages and religions. Most importantly, it urges all to unite body and mind on a higher spiritual plane in order to "know the truth of the universe".

A person whose character and identity deeply reflect this land of contrasts is Vinita Balasubramanian. Raised in a conservative Hindu family but educated in a strict Catholic convent, she experienced at an early age the contradictions of the human condition and the urgent need to overcome cultural misunderstandings. Then, newly married, she found herself in Germany with her Indian husband, learning to cope with the German way of life. Some 35 years later, with the publication of her exceptionally insightful book, *Leben und arbeiten in Indien* (Living and Working in India), she has established herself as one of the leading intercultural specialists on Indian-German relations.

Let's begin by your early experiences in life.

I was born in the south of India in Mysore but I grew up largely in the port city of Chennai, which used to be called Madras. My father worked for the railroad and was transferred quite a lot, especially in the first 12 years of my life, so we lived in several places, including the far north near Delhi.

The north is very different from the south and, if I think back, that was my first real intercultural experience. Different language, different food. Actually, if you grow up in India, you grow up multiculturally. We lived in the Moslem area of Chennai, so I woke up every morning to the sound of the mosque. My parents were fairly conservative bourgeois Hindus but they sent me to the best school in the area, a Catholic institution run by nuns. We were expected to develop our minds, not really our sense of self or any of these other things.

So, you could say it was a sort of a "let it be" philosophy that the Beatles once sang about...

Absolutely. In India one grows up learning to have a greater acceptance of differences. I went on to a Catholic university after attending an all-girls school in Chennai. All the professors were women, about a third were nuns. It had very high standards and was a no-nonsense institution. If you were doing poorly, you got a "talking to" from the nuns; if your grades didn't improve, you were encouraged to leave!

Vinita Balasubramanian grew up in a conservative Hindu household in the Moslem area of Chennai.

DANCING THE TUNE OF INTERCULTURAL SENSITIVITY

What did you study at university?

I studied English literature, then focused on Greek tragedies and especially Shakespeare during my Master's. Everything imaginable in human experience is to be found in his works: romantic love, humor, jealousy, the dark night of the soul, it's all in there. I'm still very fond of Shakespeare—every time I go to England I try to get in at least a couple of performances.

Did you speak English at home?

We largely spoke Tamil at home but English is the lingua franca in India because of all these different languages we have. If there's a party, everyone spoke English, the same held good for school and university—for me English was never a foreign language. I also had to learn the country's official language, Hindi, at school. Having a range of languages is very helpful interculturally, you become more open to the nuances of culture reflected in a language. This strikes me afresh every time I do stints working as a translator or interpreter.

    In today's world English is usually the lingua franca for intercultural teams everywhere. Team members use English flavoured with elements from their own mother-tongue and cultural values. When a German talks about *Vertrauen*, it is not exactly what an Indian means—Indians often say "faith" rather than "trust", which has different implications.

With your love of Shakespeare, how did you end up coming to Germany?

Well, right after I finished my studies, I got married. My husband was just starting a PhD in mechanical engineering in Karlsruhe and I took a German course at the Goethe Institute in Chennai. When I arrived in Germany, I could ask questions like how to get to the train station, but I didn't understand any of the answers! I was thrown into this environment where almost nobody spoke English, not even students in those days. In the mid-70s, Germany was much less open, less Americanized. There was hardly any foreign food—if you a wanted a snack, you ate *Currywurst*.

    I took some German courses at the university in Karlsruhe and qualified later to be a translator. Having learned to be systematic and disciplined, I was "up and running" in the language within a relatively short time. In the meantime, a small language school hired me, gave me exactly four hours of training, and sent me to Daimler to teach English. My colleagues and I taught groups and also gave individual lessons to executives. I was quite young and the executives were in their forties and fifties and had seen a lot of the world.

With four hours of training, how could you teach properly?

The formal teacher training followed much later. To be honest, all I did at the beginning was listen a lot. I'd offer vocabulary and correct them when needed but at the same time it was sort of like listening-therapy. I was surprised when they kept asking me to come back; this method of learning seemed to work for them. I think we underestimate the importance of being listened to attentively. After all, learning is more than just a cognitive process. It transfers best through human interaction, the "affective approach"—something which applies just as much to intercultural learning.

That's when I first realized how language impacts personality. When you speak a foreign language, it's as if you're wearing a mask. You can either talk about things that you'd never dream of talking about in your own language or feel inhibited by it.

Listening to these executives helped me to become immersed in the German mindset. Part of it comes from friends and from living in Germany, of course, but I think my depth of understanding of German mentality comes through listening and observation in a business context.

So you could say that, through a process of osmosis, you became part of the German mindset.

Absolutely. You're thinking along the same lines, not just looking in from the outside. You end up developing the German in yourself… You could say I have three little overlapping corners tucked away within me. My working persona is German, the Protestant work ethic. My thought processes are Anglo-Saxon, perhaps even Catholic, thanks to my education. And from a spiritual-emotional viewpoint, I have a Hindu-Buddhist approach. These are various facets, all of which are very useful in intercultural communication. It helps to be able to look at things from a variety of perspectives.

What was the turning point, when you started to do intercultural work, not English training?

Well, I'd like to say, strategically speaking this was the road I followed, but it didn't really happen that way. It was a twist of fate many years ago. I was part of a big group of facilitators—four in all—at a Daimler seminar called "Global Ways" for employees working worldwide. I felt I didn't know enough at all, so with my convent school training, I rushed off to the library—not Google in those days—and took out all the books I

Stuttgart-Untertürkheim, the home of Daimler, seems a proper place to learn about the German mindset…

could find. But I learnt most of all from the experience of the participants and the other facilitators—you could say it was electrifying! My formal intercultural education came later and was much less revealing.

Over the years I have held seminars and team workshops in several countries. For obvious reasons, a lot of my work is related to India and Germany. I don't have to think so hard about doing the "right" thing here—there is a high degree of instinctuality.

Where do you see the biggest issues when Germans and Indians interact?

There are the classic ones in business, which have been around for a long time. Obviously, the first one is communication. Germans often tend to find Indian communication baffling. It's a bit of a cliché that Indians never say "no" clearly but there's also some truth to it. Communication patterns can be much more diffuse in India for various reasons. One is the importance of contextuality, another is the constant fine-tuning of one's own communication to suit the expectations and responses of the partner or partners. That's hard work, believe me!

The other issue is the notion of time. Indians are said to have a cyclical rather than a linear concept of time. It's much simpler to examine the pattern of working in India. The work approach can be compared with doing a jigsaw puzzle. Indians tend to do a bit of this here, a bit of that there, then they have a cup of tea and come back to put in another piece—or take one out. At some point, let's say at the end of the week, or at the end of the month, the jigsaw, that is the project, has been completed. Germans supervising or observing this process find it chaotic—mid-way all they can see are bits of this half-finished jigsaw puzzle with huge gaps in-between, and so it's almost impossible to imagine what the finished picture is going to look like.

Finally, personal relationships and communication, which can be an issue, but which is also the solution to many of the issues. Indians are great believers in personal relationships at work. Germans tend to avoid mixing work and pleasure, they prefer to keep their relationships businesslike, their communication factual. But in India, it's a way of life—the degree of personal warmth and communication determines the success of the team. As soon as you have built up a personal relationship, communication problems disappear. Some problems, such as adherence to schedules, obviously don't disappear entirely, but the team can handle it better because they can talk about it more openly.

I was at the SIETAR congress in Berlin recently and one of its themes was "cosmopolitan communication". I felt it was an attempt to redefine a very traditional philosophical approach: if you demonstrate empathy to others, if you share human warmth, a foundation is created and no matter what the cultural background is, communication works. In Hinduism there is a belief that every human being is part of the great universal soul. If you can detect a glimmer of this universal soul in the other person, I think that's when communication begins to happen.

I find that beautifully expressed, almost poetic.

Thank you. We are not just our minds, we are not just our personalities, we are not just the culture we grew up in. We are all these things and much more than this. Perhaps what we should strive for is to act on that higher plane which connects us all—the essence of our common humanity.

Do you think this could be a way to overcome national conflicts, racism?

Perhaps not politically, but on an interpersonal level, yes. At first glance the term "racism" is a straightforward concept, often associated with white people oppressing people of other races and discriminating against them. This approach does not take human interaction—with all its attendant unpredictability—into account.

Let me give you an example from my own family at the time of the British Raj. During that period Indians were discriminated against, for example with signs outside British clubs which read "Indians and dogs not allowed". What is less known is that discrimination was also happening in reverse, i.e. practised by the Indians against the British. In those days upper-caste Indians had very strong notions of ritual impurity. For them it was unthinkable to eat or drink in the homes of the British or even touch them, like shaking hands. My grandfather, who used to work as a civil servant for the British-Indian railways, would be invited by his English bosses to their official dinners. My grandparents were happy to attend, but — they wouldn't touch any of the food or drink served there.

Now the surprising thing is that my grandfather's behavior was apparently more than just tolerated by the colonial powers that be. He continued to be invited to dinner, and rose to become the first Indian Board Member while the British were still in power. And — most surprising of all — he had a number of warm friendships with British associates which continued until well after Indian independence.

So we have institutional discrimination, i. e. British colonial rule on one hand and Indian ritual discrimination on the other. Yet, in this particular case it does not seem to have prevented a meeting of minds. I can only surmise that it worked because both sides were able to rise beyond the limitations of their particular worldviews. They were connecting on a less mundane plane, apparently on a level of empathy and mutual respect, and finding the spark that connects.

Are you saying your grandfather was an interculturalist?

In a certain sense, yes. Curiosity and openness are essential prerequisites for being an interculturalist. Though my grandfather was a strict Hindu, a very traditional man, it didn't stop him from studying Persian so that he could read Islamic literature in the original. Or requiring his grandchildren, including me, to read a verse from the Bible to him after breakfast. And willingness to learn from others. He was a stickler for punctuality, something he admired about the British. He was doing the Indian thing of assimilating.

Done wisely, assimilating is the Indian ideal, even if it does not always work in practice. You have a culture, I have a culture. The culture we are creating together is a synthesis of both. We are both constructing what is sometimes called a "third-culture reality". And when that happens, the initial cultural differences become irrelevant.

Intercultural understanding is ultimately "work in progress" created by the people involved. We as interculturalists should act as catalysts to further this process.

Well, this has been indeed a most revealing look into the Indian mindset — something very different from Western thinking. Thank you very much for sharing your thoughts and time.

It has been my pleasure.

Interview with Ida Castiglioni

Embodied ethnocentrism

Perhaps the most important value that Italians adhere to is creating the ultimate form of beauty. Known more commonly as *la bella figura,* this concept expresses an obsession with aesthetically pleasing one's senses, whether it be Michangelo's magnificent sculpture of David or simply the perfectly-matched interior of an Italian home. *Bella figura* also can be understood as making the best possible impression through appropriate behavior. Speaking gracefully and exhibiting elegance and discretion is known as "cutting a beautiful figure".

So it's perhaps no surprise that some of the most advanced research in intercultural relations—the feeling of appropriateness in a foreign setting—is coming from Italy. Otherwise known as "embodied ethnocentrism", it has become a new paradigm in the intercultural world. And one of its best proponents and theorists is Ida Castiglioni.

Born and raised in a multilingual family just outside of Milan, she intuitively sensed at a very early age that life is about having the right rhythms. Her continuing leitmotiv has been assessing the appropriate feelings for any situation. And it was no accident that, while studying international relations and cultural processes in Milan, she became a practitioner of bioenergetics, the science of energy flow in living systems, seeing it as a key to social interaction.

Dr. Ida Castiglioni teaches the sociology of cultural processes at the University of Milano-Bicocca and is a founding director of the Intercultural Development Research Institute (IDRI). She's also a certified therapist, working as an assistant faculty member at the Institute of Somatic Psychology in Milano. Author of many books and articles on interculturalism in both Italian and English, she does consulting work, conducting programs that include multicultural teamwork, global leadership and diversity training for both corporations and public institutions. And one last important aspect of her life is that she's the partner and wife of Milton Bennett.

Wishing to understand how the Italians might enrich interculturalism with their unique *bella figura* outlook, I interviewed her during her summer holidays in Portland, Oregon.

Perhaps you could tell us a little about your early formative years.

I was born just west of Milan, with parents from two different regions—my mother is from Genoa and my father from Milan. In those days, people were speaking dialects so

Milan played a central role in Castiglioni's formative years.

I grew up with two very different ones. The dialect in Genoa is almost like Portuguese while that of Milan is a derivative of French, so you could say I grew up in a multilingual environment.

This perhaps explains my strong interest in languages, which led me to study three separate languages at school. But I think the real event that led me to interculturalism occurred when I was 18. I was asked to teach Italian to a group of Japanese managers, a challenging task that lasted almost two years. It allowed me to enter a world that was far away from me, my family, my habits—it was Japan. And it was a real exchange for me because I was more interested in what they had to tell me than what I could offer them.

After that, I travelled to many places and ended up staying with a family in San Francisco. Upon returning to Milan I did an advanced degree in political science. I've always been interested in history and the philosophy of politics. Of course, when you do political science, you are exposed to a lot of international politics, international diplomacy, international history, international treaties, international everything.

How did you feel about your studies in international relations?

To be honest, I wasn't at all satisfied. The studies were miles away from experiences I'd had abroad and, in my family, we were surrounded by foreign people all the time. There was a gap, which I didn't understand then.

In any case, at the end of those studies, I ran into a program sponsored by the European Union and managed in Italy by "Intercultura". It was the first one designed for young people to become intercultural specialists, although they were called "intercultural operators". Not that multicultural issues weren't already talked about, but the idea of "intercultural" was really new. It was full theory, not to mention very thorough—eight hours a day for nine months—followed by a very interesting internship with the Irish Commission on Refugees in Dublin.

It opened a whole new world. Looking back, I'm very thankful for those days even though I probably didn't understand the importance that course would have on my life. I did it because I was interested in it, but I didn't know what was going to come next.

Afterward I did a master's degree in somatic psychology, which was not really intercultural. I'd been following bioenergetics since I was 19 and decided I wanted to become a counsellor and therapist. At the same time I was doing a post-doctorate in the sociology of social processes.

When my university created the new Milano-Bicocca campus, I was asked to help organize the sociology department, which invariably led me to becoming a faculty member. After receiving my professorship, I said to the dean, "Listen, I don't want to do academics just for the sake of saying I'm an academic. I want to open up the stream of intercultural studies that is lacking and is needed in Italy." He didn't know exactly what I meant but he was willing to say, "Go ahead, let's see what happens!"

So I was lucky enough to be among the founders of the graduate program for decision-makers in public policy and social services. We were able to establish a curriculum, which included intercultural studies. It's not only me, but also Milton and people that do intercultural pedagogy and psycholinguistics. The programs are based on real experience. Twelve years later, I'm very pleased that this program has had a real impact in Italy.

Were you working only at the university?

Oh no! The early years of academic life in Italy aren't paid. You have to pay your bills with something else and for me, that was training. By age 28 I was running lots of programs for people who needed to gain intercultural competence in Italy and abroad… from Nigeria to Norway, Eastern Europe to Mongolia! I helped support one of the biggest programs ever sponsored by the EU for former Soviet countries, which was to train junior and senior managers. And since 2009 I've been doing training programs for women, recently in Russia, Uzbekistan and the Seychelles.

One program I remember fondly was for a global corporation in Norway. As you know, the country has a huge reserve of offshore oil and the people in the industry not only come from many countries, but also from state and non-state entities with different ways of thinking. This is particularly true of the Norwegians and the Italians, who were the main stakeholders. And then all the other nationalities had to fit in. Not only power dynamics needed to be taken into account but major differences in looking at life, organizations, the position and value of work in your life. It was a huge program, lasting four years, and all the possible value contrasts you can imagine were there.

How did you go about designing the program?

The premise of the whole program was based on one question: what does it mean to be an employee of the company? We started with the idea of perception — how do you create your perception and how do you perceive and construct a different cultural identity? This was also meaningful for people who didn't have direct contact with people of different nationalities. Everybody was involved, from the operator at the front desk all the way to the top, and we had secretaries and bosses in the same class.

We first did a layer of awareness and then became more and more specialized with groups. We arrived at a point where everybody had a basic awareness, a native language they could share, and different groups could go more into depth, depending on what role they had. At this stage, I worked with them on embodiment.

You've touched on your specialty. Could you tell us some of the actual methods you used for embodiment?

The most immediate aspect of embodiment from an intercultural perspective is the feeling associated with sensing the appropriateness of certain behavior. For example, exactly when is the appropriate moment to take leave after a hosted dinner in an Italian family as opposed to a Norwegian family. Awareness or knowledge of a culture is insufficient; you need to have a feel for it. This intuitive feeling of culture is built on sensory feeling, the interface between physical sensation and conscious awareness.

The sensory feeling can be heightened by doing "breathing work". When a person deeply changes his or her way of breathing, the body faces a series of reorganizations, mostly at the neurological level. For instance, when we are exposed to an unfamiliar environment, we can intentionally change our breathing to improve our adaptation.

Through small physical movements accompanied by breathing exercises, I could make the group realize both their mental and physical agility. What I mean by agility is the ability to do context-shifting not only from a cognitive perspective but also an *experiential* perspective. How do you live your experience? With, and through, your body.

You make sense of the experience you're living at the cognitive level, but also the impulses and stimuli you're given through your body. This really changes your experience in terms of the way you can organize your perception. So what I was developing with them was two things: the feeling of appropriateness and the ability to context-shift. In the end, it means how to adapt to a different physical context and a different style not only by knowing something but also by feeling something.

All this helps you become aware of the context you're in and how to locate yourself in that context. You go from simple basic awareness to how it feels to be there. So you go from comfortable to uncomfortable to deeper issues such as acceptance or rejection of the context you're in. And then there's work on flexibility concerning things that, for instance, are not to your liking.

How did you get into this field of embodiment?

The idea of embodiment came when I was first doing my work on bioenergetic psychology. I made the connection to intercultural communication in 1997 when I was working with Milton in a course on empathy at the Summer Institute for Intercultural Communication. I said I thought there was a dimension that had been neglected for too long and was very important in how we make sense in our reality.

Over the next five years, we explored that idea as "ethnophysiology", although we don't call it that anymore. The idea is that you can be sophisticated and culturally sensitive at a cognitive level but if you don't bring your physical perceptions to that level, your body will resist. There's a trailing issue that has to do with the physical perception of that context, holding your ethnocentrism in the body.

This reminds me of modern psychotherapy, which takes the Freudian/Jungian method of being cognitively aware of your problem and combines it with physical awareness, a sort of Reichian therapy. Reliving earlier experiences is supposed to liberate patients from their neuroses.

Well, we don't want to do therapy. I'm very aware of that. Of course, when you deal with emotions, you work with a great part of the person. And when you deal with the body and the emotions embedded in the body, you're working with a greater part of that person's personality and you really have to be careful.

But we want to help people become more aware of physical cues. Doing so, they come to understand more about themselves than the context they're in. You have to use exercises that people wouldn't think about. Breathing has a major impact on the way you become aware of your body. This is true for every physical discipline related to breathing.

The point is you have people work not so much on overcoming limits but on what happens when you trespass limits. What's happening to you? How do you feel? How do you find meaning in cultural terms of that passage? How do you apply that to your work? It's actually a very powerful leadership tool.

Every time I go to Italy, I always have the impression Italians are so well dressed. And they love colors, forms, aesthetics. Your great heroes, for example Michelangelo and da Vinci, are from the world of art. Something very different from the American mindset, which is more concerned with the concrete, the pragmatic. Can you put this into an intercultural context?

First of all, you have to view Italians as having been raised with aesthetical experience. Things don't need to be perfect but there must be balance. This is sought after in the presentation of self and called *bella figura*.

I think Americans are concerned about how they look too, but they act in compartments. So, in formal or business situations, they end up wearing almost uniforms because they're taught to be a certain way and that it's the only possible way to be. Also, what I've seen in the years since I came to the U.S. is a conflict in styles.

Raphael's *Portrait of Agnolo Doni* (1505) is a timeless example of the *bella figura* concept that still is an integral part of the Italian mindset.

Americans, like Italians, enjoy shopping for fashion, particularly women. But in the U.S., there's also pressure to be loose and casual, which has almost become an imperative in the last 20 years. American women tell me, "We end up storing all these clothes in the closet. We never get to wear them because everything has become so casual." I'm not sure they're all that happy about it. The real difference is Americans don't put as much value on the way they present themselves—what they say and how they engage the discussion is more important.

In Italy, the way you present yourself shows your status. Not only what you can afford but also your social milieu: how you were raised and, above all, how you put things together. That typically tells Italians where a person is coming from and aesthetical balance really makes a difference.

How do you see the future development of intercultural research?

I personally believe that there's a lot more work that can be done, especially in reducing ethnocentrism, prejudice. And that's where embodiment comes into play. You don't do it when people are constricted by ethnocentrism, only by moving people forward and promoting ethnorelativism, where people can make sense of their intercultural experience and embodiment becomes a powerful tool.

That's what we are trying to do at the IDRI—creating critical mass to reach a deeper understanding of theoretical perspective (www.idrinstitute.org). Not to limit our options to the usual concepts that are around, but to go further, to explore physically what people wouldn't normally be aware of and, by doing so, to develop an awareness of appropriateness.

Interview with David McRae

An intercultural banker

David McRae is one of the few SIETAR members who's a banker. Drawing on a long and distinguished international career, he offers some wise lessons in intercultural relations.

Anyone who reads the papers or watches TV—which is to say pretty much everyone—can't help knowing that we're emerging from the worst global financial crisis since the Great Depression of 80 years ago.

And that, even as the world economy rebounds (according to Wall Street), unemployment is higher, with small companies continuing to go under at an alarming rate while big ones continue to lay people off. And that a record number of u.s. mortgages continue to be foreclosed by the same bankers who caused the crisis yet who, at the beginning of 2010, voted themselves billions of dollars in bonuses… Bankers have now officially out-stripped lawyers as the most vile profession in the entirety of human endeavours!

So when someone mentions an international banker who's highly sensitive to cultural differences and is, in fact, a member of SIETAR, it seems like the ultimate paradox. David McRae is no fat-cat financier, he's a true "global citizen" who's lived and worked in Asia, the Middle East, Africa, Europe and North America. He's also a history buff whose hundreds of books on the subject fill the wall-to-wall bookcases in his office. Engaging and witty, he's far more interested in discussing what makes different cultures tick than in analysing the latest stock market figures. It's this mindset that led him to become a member of SIETAR in 2001 and a strong supporter of the organization's goals ever since.

The scion of a Kipling-era British family in India, McRae was expected to go to Sandhurst, England's famous military academy. He chose banking instead, starting at Barclays at the age of 16.

At 21, he was a junior officer at the Charter Bank in Hong Kong. Then it was off to Malaysia, India, Lebanon—all this by age 30. Which is when he felt that his future lay in North America—in Canada initially. Then he went to Continental Bank in Chicago.

Ironically, this move produced a series of further international assignments—in Belgium, Greece and Canada over a 14-year period. Canada has subsequently proven to be his second home (he, his wife and son are all Canadian citizens)—and, post his formal banking career, he set out internationally again—this time as a banking consultant helping to train and coach bankers to finance small and medium-sized enterprises—in Poland, Czech Republic and Egypt—covering a 10-year spell.

David McRae has now essentially retired and lives in his wife's native country, Greece. He is, however, certainly not inactive in terms of historical studies, related travel—and his favourite sport, golf. In this interview, he talks about his long and distinguished international career and offers some wise lessons in intercultural relations.

How is it that you became so curious about intercultural relations?

I first became conscious of my upbringing when I arrived in Hong Kong. On my second day, I was invited to the British Cricket Club and there I saw an old British colonist yelling at a young Chinese waiter, "Boy, come here! Get me a drink!" I was deeply shocked by such patronizing behavior, even to this day.

A couple of years later, having been transferred to Kuala Lumpur, Malaysia, I did something that shook up the management of my bank. A Malaysian Chinese soccer team asked me to play for them and I accepted. My superiors told me not to mix with the locals—this was just not done—but I refused to back down.

To everyone's surprise, my presence on the team created such positive publicity that I was the talk of the town. My bank suddenly realized it was good public relations to mix with the Chinese!

Didn't this sort of "gone native" attitude act as a brake on your career?

On the contrary! If you want to be successful in any profession, you need to be engaged with people, all sorts of people... I've always been passionate about what I do and, whilst having dealt with large corporations extensively throughout my career, I particularly love helping entrepreneurs build small and medium-size companies. Small business creates four out of five new jobs in most free market economies!

But at the same time, I'm socially conscious. When I go to a new country, I need to connect to the "locals". It's like in rugby, you have to "rumble and tumble" if you want to understand the other players and get along with them. It's also a sport which I have enjoyed as a player and supporter over the years.

What is your method of connecting to people from other cultures?

In my mind there are three elements. First, it's most important to learn the history of a country where you're going to live. This provides a good basis for understanding the culture, which is the second thing. And third, you need to learn something of the language. Follow those rules and people will open their arms to you, no matter where you are!

In your view, what's the most common mistake expatriates make?

It's the ageless human assumption that we think people know everything we know. That's completely wrong. Early in my career I learned that the most successful expatriates are the ones who first assume differences before assuming similarity. If you have that attitude, you have a mind willing to learn more. If you think you know everything, you've stopped learning and people will sense it.

Now to a standard question — why have you continuously supported Young SIETAR?

As a member of SIETAR Europa for nine years now, I'm very cognizant of the desire of the organization to grow through an increasing number of national organizations worldwide. One good way to support this is to promote activities with younger interculturalists.

I'm particularly impressed with the enthusiasm with which the Board and its members approach the complex issues of interculturalism. I use the word "complex", given the global nature of the world today — and the problems emanating from globalization.

A final question: what's your opinion of the current global financial crisis?

The banking world has changed radically in the past 20 years or so. What's happened is that senior management gradually loosened the reins on employees and this led to a move toward esoteric products. They're so complex that those at the top have lost control. It's unfortunate but the crash of 2008 was an accident waiting to happen...

How all this will play out in the near future is difficult to say. It's not a pretty picture at the moment. The pendulum, however, will swing back again. It's human nature — people need to be controlled. We need globalized ground rules that are supportive of commerce and industry but not of reckless, casino-style trading.

Barack Obama's mind

A master of sensitivity

It goes without saying that the 21st century is a fascinating, albeit disquieting world. Old ways are being replaced by the new and this "creative destruction" has generated some interesting phenomena—one being the election of America's first black president. Not only was the election distinct, but Barack Obama's political style is different. He's described as always eager to work with friends and foes alike; at the same time he seems intellectually detached, neither here nor there... Born across boundaries, the U.S. president is a master of intercultural sensitivity, yet his intellectual detachment leads some to wonder what he believes in.

Barack Obama has often been described as the ultimate compromiser, continuously seeking to work with people on both sides of the political spectrum. When addressing controversial issues, he usually begins with a respectful nod toward the view he's about to reject—a line or two that suggests he understands and even sympathizes with the concerns of his opponents.

In *The Audacity of Hope*, he writes about trying to comprehend his adversaries' beliefs through empathy; he's willing to connect to his counterpart by intentionally shifting his frame of reference. His capacity to see and feel the relativity of beliefs, to know that there is no absolute standard of "rightness", is a clear sign of intercultural sensitivity.

At the same time, this intellectualized detachment leads some to say—often cynically—that he doesn't believe in much of anything. "No-drama Obama", the ultimate political chameleon. But where did he acquire his ability to empathize with others while remaining so detached?

Barack Obama was a child of many homes, the first modern president to have spent a good part of his childhood outside the United States. And not only did he live in Asia from age 6 to 10, his father was from Africa and his mother, America.

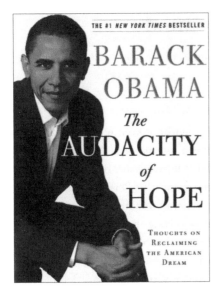

In his best-seller, Obama writes about understanding his adversary's belief through empathy.

Someone who spends part of his or her developmental years outside the "passport country" is often referred to as a third-culture kid (TCK). And children who experience abrupt changes of culture are forced to grapple with very basic questions about identity.

Imagine yourself as a six-year old living quite happily in Hawaii, then abruptly finding yourself transplanted to Indonesia and surrounded by people you can't even talk to. It goes way beyond what adults call culture shock! Just when you're coming to grips with what constitutes "normal" or "acceptable" behavior, everything is ambiguous. You've barely begun to define yourself as an individual entity on this strange planet and you're already forced to redefine yourself. The center cannot hold...

But growing up between different worlds is also a gift, generating an "ethno-relative" mindset which usually blossoms in early adulthood. Studies show that TCKs possess a high degree of social and intellectual flexibility, are quick to think outside the box and have an uncanny ability to appreciate and reconcile different points of view.

Obama's colleagues on the *Harvard Law Review* were among the first to note his exceptional skill in mediating competing points of view. (The jealous ones suggested he had a quasi-neurotic need to be liked by all sides.)

Then again, another characteristic of TCKs is detachment, sometimes perceived as being "above it all". Nearly all of Obama's classmates described him as aloof and hard to decipher. In a sense, they're not wrong: a person who looks at all angles and listens to all sides is someone whose values and norms are forever in a state of flux.

Studies show that the primary challenge for maturing TCKs is to glean a sense of personal and cultural identity from the various environments to which they've been exposed. "This is who I am, no matter where I am."

Obama's vivid memoir, *Dreams from My Father*, is a classic search for self-definition and the understanding of roots. Finding his identity proved to be extraordinarily difficult but, in succeeding, he became all the stronger.

In Obama's case, non-defined cultural identity wasn't the only problem. He was abandoned by his father, who returned to Kenya when his son was two years old, then separated from his "second father" in Jakarta when his mother sent him back to Hawaii to live with her parents when he was ten. People who lost a parent at an early age often appear cool; they don't often show emotion. It's a coping mechanism designed to get on with life "as normal". No-drama Obama is the logical consequence of childhood experience.

At the same time, one can understand his need to write *Dreams from my Father* as a healing mechanism — a way to reconnect to his African father and that African heritage, both biological and cultural.

Growing up in the USA, Barack Obama's life was also shaped by the color of his skin. Caught between the margins of White and Black America, he spent a long time wondering who he was. He was surrounded by white people in the family home but he was, himself, seen as black once he stepped outside. From age ten on, he was acutely aware of the need for dialogue between the races — even in his own family. His *Race in America* speech from the 2008 campaign mentioned his maternal grandmother's fear of black men.

Despite everything — and because of it — he managed to forge what seems to be a perfectly-balanced dual identity. It's painfully obvious that Black and White America still don't speak the same language but Mr. Obama speaks both. More importantly, he can speak *to* both. And his own "self" is far beyond the simple binary equation of black and white. It is, in fact, the most stupendous example of what interculturalist Milton Bennett calls "cultural marginality" in the history of the country!

Barack Obama might smile if he were to read what I've written thus far. "Yeah, that sort of describes my mental state…" But his remarkable upbringing definitely gave him a unique feel for a nation made up of some 200 different races. The dislocated child was free to invent a new self — a strong American theme.

Empathy combined with detachment, an insider who'll always remain an outsider at heart, a modern Soloman regarding compromises…

The problem is that such people aren't generally feared. And "other-worldly wisdom" can inspire both reverence and scorn. If Barack Obama plans to go down in history as a true leader who brought about great changes, he might want to take another look at Machiavelli:

> *If a Prince must choose to be either feared or loved, it is better to be*
> *feared, for "love is held by a chain of obligation which (for) men,*
> *being selfish, is broken whenever it serves their purpose; but fear*
> *is maintained by a dread of punishment which never fails.*

Arnold Schwarzenegger

The ultimate expatriate

One of the most interesting and potentially liberating aspects of our globalized society is expatriation. It's a process of temporarily or permanently integrating into a foreign culture. Although breaking away can be frightening and disorientating, it can also bring empathy, mutual education and, ultimately, the fascination of diversity.

Milton Bennett studied the process intensively and published the *Developmental Model of Intercultural Sensitivity* in 1986. It's a fascinating framework on how people experience cultural change, organized into a continuum of six stages. The first three are ethnocentric, meaning events and behaviors are organized and interpreted from a person's original cultural viewpoint. The last three are ethnorelative, where that viewpoint is understood in the context of a new culture.

In the final phase, "integration", a person is comfortable with multiple and often ambiguous behaviors. Bennett describes it as cultural marginality—existing on the periphery of two or more societies. Some may feel confused, even alienated, by continual transitions and develop an encapsulated marginality. Others have a conscious, pro-active attitude and build upon the excitement of complexity. Not many people reach the stage of constructive marginalization. But those who do reach this phase, have an interesting tale to tell.

The expatriate that I will introduce is a most unlikely candidate (and maybe a shock for many readers): Arnold Schwarzenegger. In the eyes of some, he's nothing more than a male chauvinist with an over-inflated ego. And his behavior for many is the quintessence of political incorrectness, thanks to his divorce in which it became known that he fathered a child with the housekeeper. Nonetheless, he's written a surprisingly insightful and well-written autobiography, entitled: *Total Recall: My unbelievably true life story*. It's the story of a young Austrian immigrant in search of the American Dream.

His story can be viewed as the apex of successful expatriation.

The reader quickly learns that Schwarzenegger possesses Herculean willpower and an absolute belief in the human spirit—his many and varied accomplishments are proof of just how far a man can go when he puts his mind to it. And childhood discipline and strenuous training as a bodybuilder informed his approach to cultural adaptation.

He spent his formative years in a small Austrian village, a few miles from Graz. He recalls how his father, an austere police chief, demanded that he and his brother do sit-ups to earn their breakfast each morning and write weekly reports on their activities with no spelling mistakes allowed. Most people would have been crippled by that kind of upbringing, he writes, but he embraced his father's attitude and turned it into a tireless, obsessive drive for success.

The thought took shape in his mind that he was special, meant for bigger things... and that those things could only happen in the USA. He sensed his destiny and, at age fourteen, started lifting weights. Six years later, in London, he became the youngest Mr. Universe ever. He won the title the following year as well, bringing him an invitation and airfare to America.

He became the greatest bodybuilder in the world, was crowned Mr. Universe seven times, but he wasn't satisfied—what he wanted was to become a Hollywood star. Agents told him his body, his accent and his name were all too weird, he'd never make it. He ignored them, worked hard on his accent, studied acting, and ultimately became one of the world's biggest box-office successes.

Another important aspect of his integration into American society was a keen sense of perception. Early on he realized the mind was like a muscle and he trained it too, determined to become "smart". He was like a sponge, absorbing everything around him, and this included cultural differences requiring reflective judgment. Throughout the book, his insights concerning the people he encounters and American culture in general will amaze most readers. What he doesn't mention, however, is that he was born with what Austrians refers to as *Bauernschlauheit,* a clever "farmer's mind".

Schwarzenegger possesses an uncanny ability to not take life too seriously, which may help explain his incredible success-story. Being neither arrogant nor overly intense was a definite advantage when he decided to go into politics. Knowing very little about issues when he first ran for governor of California, his advisors suggested he try to be witty during the debates, make people laugh. While the other candidates were shouting at each other, he'd come up with something outrageous that would have the audience roaring. People loved it and he was elected to two straight terms.

This same sense of humor allowed him to charm people from the beginning, whether in the film industry or politics, and it was one of the reasons John F. Kennedy's niece, Maria Shriver, married him. And it serves him well in interviews, as he promotes the book: he comes across as a thoughtful and sincerely compassionate individual who, despite mind-boggling success in three totally different arenas, is quite willing to laugh at himself.

Arnold Schwarzenegger represents the apex of successful expatriation. And many people without the talent and willpower of a *Terminator* manage to adapt extremely well in a new country. But Schwarzenegger's intercultural experience, because his story is unique, is uniquely entertaining.

SYNCHRONIZING BUSINESS TO CULTURAL TUNES

Interview with Geert Hofstede

The godfather of intercultural research

Thirty-five years after the publication of his revolutionary opus *Culture's Consequences,* Geert Hofstede remains a dominant influence in both the academic and cross-cultural training worlds. His research examined countries according to a series of finely-tuned dimensions—we versus I, more equal than others, he and she, avoidance of uncertainty—a radical approach which engendered an entirely new paradigm.

Firmly based in science, Hofstede's vision touched a universal nerve in its broad strokes and made the study of cultural differences far more accessible. Many people feel that no other theoretical framework goes as far in explaining how national cultures differ in terms of tolerance for ambiguity, social equality and assertiveness.

What makes his work even more fascinating is that it came about almost by accident. Hired by IBM in the mid-60s to conduct in-house "attitude surveys", he gradually began to see patterns of difference according to nationality. Corporate culture—even that of a monolith such as IBM—obviously took a back seat to the combined influences of ethnicity, geography, social values, and spiritual beliefs... but how to untangle the strands of this spaghetti-like puzzle?

Hofstede, as befits his training as an engineer and accountant, plodded along doing years of research before unveiling culture-difference analysis. No one before had empirically measured value differences among cultures and—like most people who force us to change our way of thinking—he had to battle nay-sayers. But his findings clearly showed how national and regional groupings affect the behavior of organizations, and that this is persistent across time. His insights exemplify a great mind whose independence doesn't come from ignoring rules but by organically deriving new ones.

There was criticism, of course, notably that a study of the subsidiaries of one company couldn't possibly define national cultures as a whole. But Hofstede never claimed

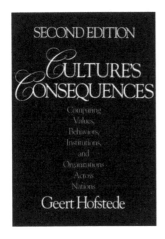

SECOND EDITION

Culture's Consequences

Comparing
Values,
Behaviors,
Institutions,
and
Organizations
Across
Nations

Geert Hofstede

His revolutionary book opened up a completely new field of study.

to do so! "I was measuring differences between national cultures, not cultures in an absolute sense…"

Because his initial work was too scientific for most people, Hofstede published a more accessible version in 1991. *Cultures and Organizations: Software of the Mind* was an instant bestseller and has so far appeared in 18 languages. His "national dimensions" have become an integral part of most intercultural programs and textbooks; his books and articles, required reading for almost any MBA or PhD program. And it is no accident that the Wall Street Journal ranked him as one of "the twenty most influential management thinkers".

I had the opportunity and privilege to meet him at his home in Velp, Holland and ask about events that helped shape his mind.

Could you give a brief description of your early life?

When the war ended in Holland in May 1945, I was due to graduate from the Gymnasium while the whole country was in chaos. The schools had been closed in the last year of the war. Despite this, the government decided to give all pupils their diploma. So I found myself, without the last year but with a diploma, entering college quite young—I was still 16.

My father, who was head of technical education in the Netherlands, suggested I should start at a technical college which had recovered from the war faster than the Technical University. I took mechanical engineering and spent my entire second year in internships—it was highly practical. I was a factory worker in various places and then I managed to get a three-month position as an assistant ship-engineer sailing from Holland to the Dutch East Indies and back.

After my internships, to avoid being drafted for military service, I didn't finish my last year of technical college but I entered Delft Technical University right away, continuing in mechanical engineering. I spent the next six years there and got involved in many other things beyond engineering.

One was becoming National President of the Liberal Christian Student Association. It was a nice time and allowed me to meet a large variety of people at other universities and widen my horizons and interests. I then became very curious about worker motivation and organization.

How did all this mix with your engineering studies?

You could say my father had a strong influence in my orientation. Although he was an engineer by training, my father was more gifted in foreign languages. In his high school days, he excelled in them and was only average in sciences. With his technical university degree he had soon become a teacher at a technical college, and he had published a much-used engineering textbook in which every chapter started with a glossary in four languages.

His main interest was not so much in technology, but in the people who do the technology and their motivation. He was known for helping academically weak children of well-to-do families. He would tell parents that their children should first master a trade, such as carpentry, to give them the experience of success, which would build up their self-confidence so that they could take advanced studies later. Many of these students afterwards thanked him for this.

So you could say my father indirectly opened other worlds than technology. The irony is that I owe my engineer-like mind to my mother, who was the technical person of the family. She was practical and would do the fixing.

It was this sort of intellectual atmosphere that broadened my mind. During my studies, I took an elective for which I had to study a book by a Jesuit, Father Kuylaars on the social role of the enterprise. Its message was that work has a double productivity: externally, to produce things and internally, to develop people. This was years before in the USA Maslow and Herzberg published their theories of self-actualization and motivation versus hygiene.

I found this fascinating and it had a great influence on me. It went along with my interest in the worker-priest (prêtre-ouvrier) movement in France, men wanted to experience the everyday life of the working class. All this provided me with the material to do a paper about work and life. By the time I finished, my interests were more in worker motivation. But mechanical engineering had disciplined my mind and that would later be very useful in my work.

After your studies, did you start as an engineer?

No, first I had to spend two years in the army. I was a technical officer in the arms-purchasing department. We were shooting and testing heavy guns and ammunition. It was adventurous, but I experienced it as a waste of time.

After that, I worked incognito as a factory worker for half a year. I did this because I wanted to know how an organization treats you when you are just seen as a worker, not as a student doing an internship. I worked with my hands and it was very, very revealing. Being a factory worker made me see things other industrial psychologists might have missed. My reports and my diary from those days were published much later in a Dutch sociology journal; an English translation has appeared in my 1994 book *Uncommon Sense about Organizations: Cases, Studies, and Field Observations.*

I got my first job as an industrial engineer in the company my father once had started working for. I was sent for a year to a consulting group to be trained in many fields: time-and-motion study, job classification, quality engineering, personnel selection. I became an internal consultant for the company. Later on, I was sent on a ten-week management course, one of the first in the country. We were sixteen young academics from different companies and by the end of the course we knew each other pretty well, including our strengths and weaknesses, our responsibilities and our salaries. It was there that I realized I could do something else, and I left the company pretty soon afterwards.

I was hired as a future plant manager in a hosiery factory. That was a disaster—I ended up getting fired along with another manager—but it was a good experience; I learned a lot about people and Machiavellian power-politics.

My next job was in a textile company that needed to be modernized. They hired a former professor of economics as a financial director, who took me on as his assistant. However I already knew I wanted to do something else, get training in social science. The professor, who was very open, made a deal with me: you help me transform the company for two years and, afterwards, I'll allow you to do a doctorate while working half-time.

The only requirement to do a doctorate in Holland those days was to write the thesis. I didn't have to attend classes but I had to turn myself into a psychologist and that meant reading and studying many, many books.

So that meant self-teaching?

Yes, you could say I was a self-learner. And there was a lot of pressure because my wife and I had a growing family; I was working half time and studying. But I managed to do my doctorate in an incredibly short time—two and a half years—and even got a cum laude.

What subject did you write on?

My thesis was *The Game of Budget Control.* It was in English, which in Holland was un-usual in those days. I chose the theme because during my time with the textile company, we had been setting up a budget system. My focus in that process had been on people's behaviour. For the thesis I did extensive interviewing and some surveying in six other Dutch manufacturing plants. The message in the thesis is that for a budget to be motivating, you should allow a margin of play or game in it. A commercial edition of my thesis was published in the UK and it became quite popular among accountants and led to a new field of study—behavioral accounting. You could say I was more or less the founding father and I even got one of my honorary doctorates for it.

His doctor thesis is now regarded as a classic in the accounting field.

So, you're also an accountant!

Well, in a way. In fact I gave a speech last year at an international accountants' workshop.

When you finished your PhD, you joined IBM?

Yes, the textile company wasn't doing too well and IBM offered me a position in their international executive development department. I would also have to coordinate personnel research in the European subsidiaries. As a product of the Dutch school system of the 1940s, I could converse with people in Dutch, English, French, German and Italian, which came in very useful. We set up a system of periodic attitude surveys among IBM employees worldwide, and I had to use all my sales skills to convince local general managers to participate.

I worked with bright American and European colleagues who were very willing to share insights and observations. We made a fine team. I had my finest hours at IBM and made many friends in the company. I even received an award for the work I did.

How did this work with attitude surveys lead to your breakthrough on cross-cultural dimensions?

In six years of working with people and with surveys in different places, I had noticed differences between countries but not completely understood the reason for them. The year 1968 brought its student revolts in several European countries and I noticed differences in the IBM subsidiaries in employees' ways of dealing with power and powerlessness. I wanted to analyse more.

IBM generously granted me a two-year sabbatical to teach and do research at IMD (then called IMEDE) in Lausanne. When I was due to return, I proposed to IBM to continue my research into national differences. Unfortunately I had got a new boss, who had no feeling or perspective on what I did, and wanted to assign other priorities. He said I could give my research material to a university. Being somewhat stubborn, I said I would join that university, and consequently left IBM in 1973, with the permission to carry the survey results with me for further analysis.

I got a part-time teaching job at the INSEAD in Fontainebleau and a research position at EIASM (European Institute for Advanced Studies in Management) in Brussels. This allowed me to continue my research into national differences. The process took six years. I began to intensively read anthropology, international economics, world literature—I'd read anything in order to make sense of the results I had.

I finally published my findings and conclusions in *Culture's Consequences* in 1980. The rest, as you know, is history.

One last question: If you were a young researcher today, what intercultural issues would you investigate?

Follow your own interests and instincts. Talk from the heart. The ones who have the best chance to make a difference are those with something to tell based on their own experiences and relationships.

Interview with Nancy Adler

A pioneer in cross-cultural management

When it comes to social change, California has been at the forefront of new American life-styles for half a century. The Golden State was relatively conservative—even complacent—until the 1960s, then "sex and drugs and rock and roll" changed everything.

The revolution was musical, first and foremost, because the music conveyed the message and the message was political. The first televised war in the history of the world resulted in a peace movement which stretched from San Francisco–Berkeley to London, Paris and… Prague.

Nancy Adler was also living in California; she was in her teens, practicing classical violin after school. Her mother's Viennese culture, rooted in intellectual rigor and perseverance, was—happily—coupled with the American revolutionary spirit of innovation. Her perspective was influenced by this California culture she grew-up in: "laid-back" values, combined with a striving for excellence, that has led to innovation and, in some cases, radical change. In her family's home, the music of the Beach Boys and The Doors played against a backdrop of a classical music. The result was to be her pioneering work in cross-cultural management.

Forty years ago, cross-cultural management was virtually an unknown field. It was widely assumed that American techniques were state-of-the-art and therefore could be applied to run any company anywhere in the world; saying otherwise was tantamount to heresy.

In the mid-1970s, Nancy Adler was beginning her PhD in management. She already sensed that global complexity couldn't be reduced to American assumptions of universality. She began researching how culture affects global business behavior and chose to write her doctoral thesis on re-entry transitions.

McGill University

Her research was highly praised, leading several U.S. universities to offer her a professorship... on the condition that she agree not to teach "that intercultural stuff" to their students. But McGill University—in bilingual, bicultural Montreal—appreciated the importance of her work. McGill hired Nancy to teach cross-cultural management, an approach that has since become a staple of MBA programs worldwide.

Her first book, *International Dimensions of Organizational Behavior,* hit the mark. A million-seller, now in its fifth edition, it's become the standard reference on how the various dimensions of culture impact the managers' and organization's behavior worldwide.

Adler went on to conduct research on female leaders—presidents and prime ministers of countries and CEOs of global firms—as well as on what supports successful cross-cultural leadership. In a highly unusual convergence, she now integrates artistic approaches into management education and executive seminars. Drawing on her passion for painting, she found that art allows managers to reflect, to move beyond the "limiting, dehydrated language and behavior of traditional management".

Author of ten books and more than 125 articles, Adler is also a first-class communicator. She was named "Outstanding Senior Interculturalist" by SIETAR in 1991 and has received McGill's Distinguished Teacher in Management award... twice!

Wanting to know more about what made her atypical, I began the interview with her early upbringing...

What experiences in your childhood steered you into the intercultural field?

In order to understand my interest in intercultural studies, you have to view both sides of my family. My mom is from Vienna and my father is American, which meant I grew up in an intercultural home.

I remember one particular incident when I was just starting elementary school. On the first day, like the rest of the children, I brought my lunchbox. My favorite sandwich was pumpernickel bread with cream cheese and olives. I sat down for lunch with the other children and they all started laughing at me because I was eating a dark bread sandwich. All of the other children had white bread sandwiches with peanut butter and jelly or baloney.

I returned home upset because my classmates were laughing at me and my sandwich. So my mother, who wanted me to be happy, bought white bread and peanut butter and jelly. At school the next day, I proudly took out my sandwich, ate my first bite, and immediately decided it tasted awful.

After school that day, I told my mom I hated the white bread. She responded by saying, "OK, what you need to do tomorrow is explain to your friends that dark bread is 'very special bread'." The new description worked instantly. Now the other children all wanted to taste my special black-bread sandwich. From then on, my mother had to send me to school with extra sandwiches!

My mother, being an immigrant, figured out what I needed to do to fit in. Not going into the melting-pot; I was not going to attempt to be exactly like "the locals". Rather, the question was, how can I stay me without threatening the other children? From the perspective that you and I have today, we can easily decode what was going on. What I was doing was taking a foreign object (black bread) and explaining it to "the natives". As opposed to them continuing to think that black bread was weird and awful, I (with the help of my mother) turned the bread into something special. The children immediately became comfortable with it; the bread was now interesting, rather than "foreign".

Were there other intercultural experiences?

There were many. Because my mother was Viennese, the arts and culture were very important to her. Although my family didn't have much money (and certainly not enough to spend on symphony tickets), my mother discovered that the Los Angeles Philharmonic offered free dress-rehearsal concerts on Wednesdays that she could take my sister, brother and me to. None of the neighborhood kids had ever gone to a classical music concert, so she always invited some of our friends! Once again, it became a special adventure—going to hear classical music—at a time when classical music was certainly not part of mainstream California culture.

Both my sister and I took violin lessons, starting when we were very little. The talent, however, went to my sister. She became quite good and her son is now a professional violinist. My mother also regularly took us to art museums. Those experiences influenced me profoundly, as I am now both an artist and a professor. From an intercultural perspective, my mother was constantly capturing what was precious about having grown up in Vienna and passing it on to us within the context of America's culture.

Being polite and speaking correctly is another example of an early childhood influence. In general, there is a higher level of formality in Europe than in the United States. As children, we were taught to speak correctly and politely, in a way that is more common in Europe than in California. A constant refrain in our home was, "Don't use the word 'yeah'. Civilized people don't speak like that!" In our home, any time you said "yeah" instead of yes, you had to put a penny in the small jar my parents had placed on the table The rule applied to our friends as well as to us. Every few months, my parents would buy us ice cream or something else special with the money. Although this was the opposite of California's informal culture, all our friends knew that they needed to use proper language in our home.

Reflecting on my childhood, I realize that it gave me a good grounding for my later writing and speaking. Today, when I lecture to international groups, they often comment that I'm easy to understand. I don't tend to use contractions or slur my words. It comes in part from learning English from my mother, who spoke it as a foreign language.

Would you say this contributed to you receiving two Professor-of-the-year awards?

That explains part of it, but, if I were to use our cross-cultural vocabulary, I'd say that the more important piece is making ideas easy to understand. Luckily, I was coached that the most important aspect of teaching is what people understand and learn, not simply what is presented. So, instead of acting like a more traditional academic ("I'm smart about this topic and I'm going to give you a lecture on what I'm smart about"), I always try to start with what the audience is most interested in; what they have questions about. I try very hard to use everyday language rather than academic jargon.

Using the terminology of "push-pull", I try to create pull strategies. Ideally, the audience should want to pull from me what they most want to learn, rather than me attempting to simply push what I know towards them. I therefore often use questions—similar to the way you started this interview (with "Why would a child steer toward the cross-cultural?") The art is to have the audience ask itself, "What cross-cultural skills do I need?"—"What can I contribute to the world using my cross-cultural skills?"

I wrote *International Dimensions of Organizational Behavior* for the first cross-cultural course I taught at McGill in the early 1980s. Each chapter was a module in the seminar. When I designed the course, I imagined that the people listening to my lectures and reading the book were intelligent people who knew absolutely nothing about the topic. It was my job to get them excited and knowledgeable about cross-cultural management.

This is quite different from traditional university teaching.

Yes, it is. Perhaps this is another influence of California culture. California traditionally has had considerably less hierarchy—with more of a learning culture than an expert culture—both in comparison to much of Europe and to traditional academia. It is not surprising that Silicon Valley flourished in California.

I was raised and educated in California. I received all three of my university degrees from the University of California at Los Angeles (UCLA). During that entire period, I was inside of California culture. I remember taking a freshman course at UCLA called *The Jew and the Changing American Society*. The course, with hundreds of students enrolled, was presented by a psychologist, a sociologist, a historian and a rabbi. Their purpose was to give us skills at making sense of contemporary society. It wasn't a traditional course in which students assume that the professor (or the textbook writer) already knows all the answers. Rather, the fundamental premise of the course was a question: how do we understand contemporary society? Everyone contributed their expertise and perspective, professors and students alike, to try to help us collectively make sense of reality.

You did your PhD on the re-entry process, which in the mid-70s was an unknown topic. Could you tell us a little more about how you came to focus on that topic?

In the 1970s, the field of intercultural management didn't exist. The only international management topics that were taught were international finance and marketing. For instance, at a very basic level, international marketing taught that, with the advent of competition from Fuji, Eastman Kodak needed to use the local language on their film boxes in non-English speaking countries. Very, very basic understandings.

At that time, international organizational behavior wasn't taught. Cross-cultural leadership, cross-cultural team building, cross-cultural negotiations... none of these fields existed. However, even though the field did not yet exist as an academic discipline, my MBA experience as an intern with the Ministry of Culture in Israel (and then getting caught in the Yom Kippur War), left me highly motivated to figure out how cross-cultural interaction and transitions really worked.

When I suggested doing my doctoral dissertation on re-entry—on how to manage the cross-cultural transition back home from a foreign assignment—UCLA's management faculty was surprised. Nobody had ever conducted a study on re-entry. The cross-cultural literature at the time focused primarily on outbound transitions and cultural shock. UCLA made a deal with me: I could study re-entry if I also became an expert on research methodology. UCLA assumed that if I was going to research a topic that was so new that it didn't even exist yet, then it was particularly important that I become knowledgeable in the best available approaches to research. So I became well-trained in both quantitative and qualitative methodology, which has served me very well throughout my career.

I formed my PhD committee with professors with a broad range of expertise. I chose a top international business professor, a cross-cultural psychologist, an anthropologist, and even went to the East-West Center in Hawaii to study with Richard Brislin, one of the luminaries of cross-cultural studies. At that time, the cross-cultural knowledge that was beginning to come into management was primarily comparative. The very notion of intercultural interaction, rather than comparison, that I was interested in, simply didn't exist.

The field's emphasis on comparison was understandable, but not helpful. Early academic studies on international organizational behavior were based primarily on anthropology. Anthropologists' models have historically been primarily descriptive or comparative. Anthropologists usually ask the question "How can we understand the people who live in this particular place?" Anthropologists rarely investigate what happens when people from one culture interact with those from another culture.

So, if I understand you correctly, you were increasingly moving toward what we today would label as intercultural questions — "How can people from around the world work effectively together?"

Correct. I was not simply interested in "How do we understand people from other cultures?" I wanted to know how people from different parts of the world could succeed in getting things done together. How could they negotiate together? How could they work effectively in teams together? What kinds of leadership worked best when teams included people from various cultures?

I was strongly drawn toward management models because business has the overarching goal of getting done what needs to get done. There has been stronger pressure on business to interact effectively cross-culturally than on other sectors of society. The business model invokes such questions as: "OK, if, as a European company we are merging with a Japanese firm, how do we get the work done?" The underlying assumption is that there is always an answer; the challenge is to find it.

Let's turn to "International Dimensions of Organizational Behavior". Were you thinking of writing it when you started at McGill?

No, the concept for the book came about accidently. I was invited to my first Academy of International Business meeting and my new colleagues introduced me to David Ricks, editor-in-chief of the *International Dimensions* book series. When he learned I was developing a cross-cultural management course, he invited me to write a book on international organizational behavior. The first edition was published in 1985. Initially, it had no competition, as there was no field yet. Perhaps the reason *International Dimensions of Organizational Behavior* has done so well over the last 25 years is its message: that we all need to transcend parochialism—no matter which country we come from—and see the world from a global perspective.

What do you feel are the challenges facing the SIETAR movement in our globalized world?

It's a fabulous question. I think an analogy is the pumpernickel sandwich I described earlier. For many people, when they hear the term cross-cultural, they confuse melting-pot and domestic-multiculturalism strategies. So, the first question for SIETAR and the field is clarity: what is the field aiming at? Is it aiming at everybody attempting to be the same? Or at everybody, no matter how different they are, being able to live and work successfully together? Those are two very different models. SIETAR's primary contribution has been in using the latter perspective.

The second fundamental cross-culture challenge for SIETAR and the field is: How do societies recognize differences and use them to build something better—better teams, better organizations, better communities, better countries, and a better world. Implicit in that challenge is the need for education. Today, both in Europe and North America, issues of class and politics are confounded with cultural dynamics. Many immigrants, due to class and poverty issues, have not had access to adequate education, language learning, or good jobs. That does not mean that immigrants cannot contribute. It does mean that people without access to society's resources, including, most fundamentally, a good education, find it very difficult to contribute, no matter who they are.

Once a society establishes inclusive systems of good education, including the learning of languages, it can focus on supporting people in working effectively together. We need to ask what we, as a global society, can learn from the communities in which inclu-

Nancy Adler sees each of her artistic pictures as "an invitation to reflect on the world from a new perspective".

sive strategies have worked? If, for example, we were to study Sarajevo prior to the invasion by outside forces, we would immediately learn that it had one of the most positive networks of relationships among Christians, Muslims and Jews, with the three religious communities successfully working together within individual institutions and the community as a whole. It was fabulous, yet much of the world fails to recognize why it was so successful.

We have a dangerous tendency to blame problems on others, and in particular, on those we consider "outsiders". In the economically privileged countries of Europe and North America, for example, we have seen an increase in the popularity of anti-immigrant sentiment and legislation. In most cases, "blame" masquerades as problem solving. The question we need to ask ourselves is "How do we, as a global society, achieve and maintain inclusive lifestyles in flourishing societies?" It's dysfunctional to blame and counterproductive to accept such simplistic statements as "The reason we're losing ground is because of immigrants" as problem-solving.

I'm thinking along the same lines. My feeling is that economically advanced societies aren't really willing to put in the effort and resources to make multiculturalism work. Those in power say, "No, we can't afford that. We aren't going to raise taxes for these immigrants!"

Unfortunately, such attitudes are riddled with fallacious thinking. They assume, for instance, that immigrants will simply go back to where they came from and not cause "my country" any more problems. Similarly, they assume that rising unemployment and levels of violence in one country will stay in that country and not impact their neighbor's economy or society. As country after country is discovering, the assumption that isolation will cure everything may have worked in the 19th century, prior to global interconnectivity, but such assumptions and the behaviors they foster no longer work in the 21st century.

What would you recommend SIETARians do?

I would say again what I recommended at the end of the speech I gave at the SIETAR Europa Congress in Granada: "Intercultural skills are more important today than they have ever been before."

Multiculturalism is not simply about understanding: "Oh, I recognize you're different; that's okay, you're nice." Rather, it requires that we ask the question "What is the advantage of working together with people who are different from me?"—"How do we leverage our differences to the benefit of all of us?" For the world to thrive, it no longer has a choice not to succeed at multiculturalism.

Unlike what some politicians would have us believe, we cannot throw out the cultural diversity that exists in the world, nor make people who are different from us disappear. We cannot throw out immigrants and assume that we will have a successful society. That's not an equation that has worked or will work; it is founded on a fundamentally false premise.

One of the next steps for SIETAR is to consistently adopt a multi-level perspective, simultaneously considering events and dynamics from the perspective of the world, region, country, and organization, team and individual.

SIETAR has tended to be better at offering explanations for working effectively at the micro (individual) level; and at developing skills for individuals and teams. SIETAR has focused less frequently on developing the skills and understanding needed for working successfully with organizations and their overall strategy, with countries in achieving their overall goals, and with what is the most important for the world as a whole. There is no question that if SIETAR broadens its emphasis on historic, micro-level competencies, it can make significant contributions in the 21st century.

If, however, SIETAR remains circumscribed at the micro-level, it risks becoming irrelevant. That would be a shame, since, to state it from the perspective of a kindergartner: the world needs people to learn to play nicely with each other.

Interview with Fons Trompenaars

Gaining synergetic sophistication

Anglo-Irish playwright Oscar Wilde famously stated, "I can resist everything except temptation." This little phrase summarizes an ageless human dilemma: how do we deal with the contradictory forces within ourselves?

On the whole, people in the West have been taught not to waste time with eccentric riddles; life is serious and should be treated with Cartesian "either-or" logic. And the bi-polar mindset worked fairly well in the industrialized world until the dawn of globalization. From then on, however, people (and companies) were continually confronted with bizarre codes of behavior.

It didn't take long for individuals like Fons Trompenaars to look for ways to reconcile seemingly incompatible cultural traits. Born and raised in a Dutch-French family, he understood the contradictory lifestyles of Amsterdam and Paris and eventually wrote a doctoral thesis on the effect national culture has on corporate culture. Generating seven dimensions, he detailed how groups often hold values that are mirror images of one another.

He later teamed up with Charles Hampden-Turner to write the best-seller *Riding the Waves of Cultures* which identifies seven "opposing" value dimensions and the problems they create, then suggests solutions that often foster wealth-building. While scholars point out that the work is not as rigorous as that of a Geert Hofstede, it has become a major reference. The humorous, easy-to-read style and the countless case studies examined make it a highly stimulating must-read for those in international business.

Fons Trompenaars' landmark research in international management has him very much in demand all over the world. Getting a hold of him wasn't easy but thanks to the advances of smart-phone technology, I was able to share an early-morning (virtual) coffee with him in Barcelona.

What childhood experiences led you to the intercultural field?

Having a Dutch father and a French mother, my brother and sisters and I learned to shift between the two cultures and considered them equally real. Our summers were spent with my grandparents near Paris and two uncles, an aunt and seven cousins also lived

The grand manoir in Paris, where Fons Trompenaars spent his summer holidays.

there. It was a huge house with great feeling. It was also interesting as the subculture of families was so different in France.

Everyone sat down for two warm meals a day together, which wasn't very Dutch. And it tasted good, which wasn't very Dutch either! And there was wine at the table, which was a no-no in Holland.

One time I went to France alone and when I came back I forgot to speak Dutch to the taxi driver — I was really inundated by French culture. It also came with problems. When I was 18 or 19, I was still living with my parents and my Dutch friends at university had all moved out of the house. I knew I couldn't do the same out of respect for my mother.

So those early experiences laid the foundation. But what exactly pushed you into a lifelong career of cross-cultural research?

It happened accidently. I studied economics with a major in organizational behavior. When I finished at the Free University of Amsterdam in 1978, one of my professors told me about a PhD scholarship in the States. I was fairly young and decided to try. The jury consisted of top professors from all over Europe: André Laurent, Geert Hofstede, Giorgio Inzerilli, Gunnar Hedlund. I hardly knew them. Anyway, to cut a long story short, the jury gave me the scholarship. Afterwards both Laurent and Hofstede said, "For your PhD, why don't you look into the cultural side at the Wharton Business School in Philadelphia?"

Having been raised in a Dutch–French environment, everything fell into place. Laurent with his French enthusiasm encouraged me to go into this field and Hofstede handed me a pack of articles. I loved reading them and thought his work was fascinating. That's when I got the cultural virus. My idea was to write a thesis, entitled "The organization of meaning, the meaning of organization." The organization of meaning being culture, and the meaning of organization being corporate culture. So my dissertation was about how national culture affects corporate culture.

On the cultural side, I developed something, based on Max Weber's thinking and Toennies' *Gesellschaft und Gemeinschaft,* that I called left-brain versus right brain. And for corporate culture, I took Hofstede's *Four Dimensions.* Hofstede was not known at that time and the panel asked me to defend his concept. So I went back to Hofstede, to whom I owed a lot, and asked "Why those four dimensions?" His answer was simple—he got angry.

It was obviously the weakness of his research; it was not deductive, but inductive. His work was based on other types of research at IBM that he statistically analyzed. That was the sensitive point. Hofstede has been very important for the field of cross-cultural management because he started it, but he also closed the field. If you are in multicultural management, you should be open to other approaches. If people criticize my work I usually learn something. The trouble with Hofstede is that you can't have a discussion with him.

So I had to develop my own stuff. I took Hofstede's work and added that of others. If you want my deeply scientific discourse on how I came to the *Seven Dimensions,* it's simple. I took all the existing models, many overlapping, put them into a basket, shuffled them and came up with the seven that are always mentioned: Parsons, Hall, Hofstede, Kluckhohn, Strodtbeck.

As for my research, it was comparing Shell refineries throughout the world. I received a scholarship from the company but they didn't interfere with my work. I developed my own questions and tried not to be ethnocentric. I had my questionnaire tested by multicultural groups and what we call focus groups today. I also used existing parts of questionnaires on, for example, internal and external control, the validates locus control questionnaires by Julien Rotter and so on.

What did you do after finishing your doctorate?

I worked in Human Resources at Shell in their main office in Rotterdam and the Research Center in Amsterdam from 1982 to 1989. The latter was a big organization with 2200 people of 30 different nationalities. I later wrote *Managing People Across Cultures,* a look at how the company adapted to cultural differences.

I continued my research there. For example, I examined how two social researchers at Shell had developed the HAIR L system. "H" stands for helicopter quality, the ability to look beyond the problem (see the big picture), then land on the problem (see the details), a sort of lateral thinking. "A" stands for power of analysis, "I" for imagination, "R" for a sense of reality and the "L" at the end for effective leadership. All the bosses and managers were graded on these five basic qualities, what are now called competencies. And when we recruited people, we looked at their currently estimated potential (CEP), the job group they'd belong to at 50.

I correlated the five appraisal qualities with the people's potential. If you do straight correlation, everything correlates so you have to do multi-variate analyses, to arrive at partial correlations. In the Netherlands only analysis and imagination correlated and imagination correlated negatively. I remember my first boss at Shell who said, "Fons, you are OK. But there's only one problem—you score very high on imagination and that is very bad for your career at Shell."

The company was essentially saying imagination was bad for potential. Cynics would say, "Imagination will make you a great researcher, but not a good manager." We found that imagination scored much better in France. Analytical ability also scored high in France but the sense of reality was low. In Germany, on the other hand, leadership scored the highest. So the system is culturally biased. What do you do if people in the London or The Hague headquarters look at a wonderful French candidate, but find he scores high on imagination? French management appreciates this trait but the British and Dutch look at each other and think, "We can't move him to the next level."

I could explain this sort of behavior with my research, Geert Hofstede's research, Andre Laurent's research, Edward Hall's research, all the research, but the question became "So what?" In other words, what do we do now? I think the big problem in our field is we see the world on a bi-polar scale. Everybody's great at explaining why people are different and why something doesn't work but they don't have a clue how to make it work.

So what did you do to resolve this problem?

I think we are getting into the core, where my calling is. While at Shell I read an article by Charles Hampden-Turner, one of their consultants. *A Tale for Two Paradigms* was a bit about East versus West and ended with, "It creates dilemmas. What can we do to reconcile those dilemmas?" This five-page article not only summarized my four years of research and my dissertation but also went far beyond it.

I sent Charles my thesis and he came back a few days later and said, "I think we can work together. I reconciled all of your seven dilemmas." I said to myself, "What the hell is this guy saying?" And he gave me a crystal-clear example, asking why an individualist couldn't be a collectivist at the same time.

"If you an individualist without collectivism, you're an egoist and it doesn't work. If you're a collectivist with connecting yourself to an individual, you're a communist and it doesn't work." The meaning of life is in how you combine opposites. Great individuals are individualists and offer the fruits of individual greatness to the team. And great teams are those, which nurture individual excellence. Why don't we measure how good nations are by connecting opposites? It took me 15 years to really understand that.

Could you explain in more detail what you mean by combining opposites?

Charles Hampden-Turner

We have made the world bi-polar. Take the Myers-Briggs questionnaire, which has four categories: introvert–extrovert, thinking–feeling, judging–perceiving, sensing–intuitive. There are observable differences in personality according to national origin. The predominant type in British management ist ISTJ (Introverting, Sensing, Thinking, Judging), while in the U.S. it's ESTJ (Extroverting, Sensing, Thinking, Judging).

Myers-Briggs fans find solutions in the team, complementarities of types, or they refer to the fact that the types are only preferences and all is potentially within the individual.

But why were the questionnaires designed on mutually exclusive values in the first place? Our Western way of thinking is based on Cartesian logic: "either-or", not "and-and". This is in contradiction to what Carl Jung had in mind when he construed the underlying conceptual framework behind MBTI.

Any Myers-Briggs person I meet, I ask, "Does scoring high on thinking mean I need to score low on feeling? Why is my thinking done at the cost of my feeling? And why should I score low on collectivism if I score high on individualism?"

Take the U.S. It's very individualistic on every score but if you look at volunteer work and community groups, it's great. Icons like Bill Gates and Ted Turner make a lot of money but they also give back to society.

This is the paradigm I used at Shell. If you have imagination, it's the vertical bar on the grid, the y-axis. Sense of reality is the horizontal axis. You measure people on the combination. A person with imagination but no sense of reality is a "daydreamer". A sense of reality with no imagination makes you a "landed mole". We made grids for analysis and synthesis, as well as intuitive and sensing and it worked everywhere: great leaders are those who combine. That's true in Germany, in France, in America, even in Japan.

Coming back to my original example of the French candidate, his challenge is to go from imagination to reality. For the Dutch, it's the other way around. We call it dilemma reconciliation.

Do you see interculturalists moving toward dilemma reconciliation?

Not really. I live in Amsterdam where 60% of people under 18 don't have Dutch parents. So the majority is diverse — Dutch, Moroccan, German, Turkish, Italian, what have you. We can explain, Turks are like this, Moroccans are like that. So what? What we need is a paradigm that connects them. That's what my company is all about. When we do our workshops, participants say "Wow, dilemma reconciliation is what we need!" Clients understand we not only offer a model for showing differences, but an approach toward dealing with the difference.

I have to laugh when I go to conferences; it's all about what's the best model. And I'm thinking "Are you still at that stage? You still don't get it?"

In my opinion, if you look at our field in the last 30 years there hasn't been a major breakthrough in thinking. In academia, it's peanuts what they do today. They quote each other in great admiration and don't allow any criticism.

What we need is to have a fundamental discussion on how we can get the bi-polar models into a third way of combining. Who cares what model you use. Give me insights on how to deal with the differences. I would love to discuss what is the best model and it will be a wonderful discussion. But I also want to have a discussion on what are the next steps. Third-culture reality is dilemma reconciliation.

We had a time where the half logics we developed in the U.S., France, Nigeria and Japan were OK for local people because they stayed home. Today we need to develop a paradigm that works in multi-cultural groups. We have to go beyond linear thinking and think about how to develop trans-cultural competence, the competence to recognize, respect, reconcile and realize cultural differences. A competence model that doesn't include the competence to connect different viewpoints is useless.

How does SIETAR fit into all this?

I think SIETAR can play a very important role but it should go beyond following an existing pattern. I went to a national SIETAR event recently and was dumbstruck at how people are still explaining cultural differences. It's a bit like going to a doctors' conference where they all smoke. I told them they had to become more effective at dealing with those differences. Cultural awareness helps but let's not exaggerate its importance.

In SIETAR we need to practice what we preach. We need to say, "It's wonderful to have different viewpoints. Let's combine them and reconcile dilemmas."

We have responsibilities to the world. All the problems we are facing—wars, religious conflicts—have to do with intercultural issues. Let's have a good discussion and let's not exclude people. Even if you don't reconcile all the dilemmas, at least you're in a dialogue between cultures. In the long run, it will certainly help.

Last question: Is there anyone else who has been a source of inspiration, apart from the intercultural thinkers?

I often write with Neil Young's music in the background. The combination of hard rock, soft acoustics and great lyrics is overwhelming. I had the privilege of meeting him on the boardwalk in Santa Cruz in 1978 and after a concert in Rotterdam three years later. In 2001 I gave him the first copy of *21 Leaders for the 21st Century*—it's dedicated to the "ever inspiring" Mr. Young.

There's also the British film actor John Cleese. We did a series of workshops together for a few years and he taught me that humor is essentially the result of two opposing logics, both becoming logical. It's an important message for organizations like SIETAR.

Interview with Peter Franklin

Researching intercultural management

The study of intercultural management—how people of different cultural backgrounds come together and "make a deal work"—has become an important and exciting field of research. And rightly so—with the exponential growth of globalization, there has been a demand for a more systematic understanding of the diversity and complexity of people's behaviors.

Intercultural management is continually evolving and certainly more sophisticated than it was 30 years ago. Then, researchers naively assumed that work behavior was universal—what was true for Americans was also true for people from other countries working worldwide. We now know this was fundamentally wrong. Although cultural differences are often hard to decipher, and may appear bizarre at first, we've learned that cross-cultural management works. But it requires developing a profound and dialectic understanding of attitudes, thinking patterns and behavior. In short, intercultural competence.

One person who seeks to advance our knowledge while developing the best practices for international managers is Peter Franklin. Professor at the Konstanz University of Applied Sciences and co-author of the books *The Mindful International Manager* —an expanded edition was published in 2014—and *Intercultural Interaction,* he's a British national who is perfectly integrated in the German academic world. He created and manages the highly-acclaimed "dialogin.com" website as well, providing interculturalists with a platform for forums, book reviews and articles. With a bilingual family, he thrives at juggling British and German values—an interculturalist par excellence.

Wanting to know more about Peter Franklin's background and his on-going activities, I visited him at his home in a village on the banks of Lake Constance.

Let's begin with your roots. What were the early experiences which connected you to the intercultural field you were later to enter?

Well, I was born in the port town of Dover in southeast England. We lived in Deal, a few kilometers up the coast. On a clear day we'd look across the English Channel and say, "Oh, you can see France today." I suppose the continent of Europe was more present in that respect in my daily life as a child than for many other Brits.

My parents were open to the outside world, though they themselves had very little foreign experience. I remember my mother spoke interestingly of a school exchange with Dortmund in Germany she took part in during the Nazi period, my father was in Norway with the British army at the end of the Second World War but otherwise my parents were themselves unfamiliar with foreign countries. Still, they obviously thought contact with other cultures was important because they encouraged me to take part in two school exchanges with the city of Koblenz. This certainly influenced my subjects at A-level, when I chose English, French and German.

I was accepted at Cambridge University where I studied modern and medieval German, Swedish and English. I expressly chose Swedish because I wanted the experience of learning a foreign language from zero as an adult. I knew what it was like to learn French and German as an eleven-year-old but at 18, you approach the task in a different way. So, just before beginning my studies I went to Sweden for six weeks to start learning the language.

Then I went to West Berlin for four months. This was in 1974 and it was an absolute eye-opener for a young man like me. I got to know the German way of life and spent a lot of time going to concerts and plays—and bars and pubs. And I worked in the men's department of the Wertheim department store on Kurfürstendamm selling shirts and ties, my first real intercultural experience! I acquired an interesting specialised vocabulary relating to shirt sizes and styles!

How did you get into intercultural teaching and research in Germany?

That's a question I ask myself at times. You could say that my interest in interculturalism developed through a number of chance events.

While I was at Cambridge, I decided to spend a year in Innsbruck, Austria, working as a foreign language assistant. Like many other language teachers, I had this belief that successful cross-cultural communication simply depended on a good mastery of the language. Very quickly, I learned otherwise. That year teaching English to Austrian children was a wonderful experience and made me realize that teaching was what I wanted to do. So, after finishing my studies, I took a job teaching English at a language school in Cologne. My plan was to stay in Germany for two years but, after 18 months, I received an offer to teach English and cultural studies at the Aachen Technical University. That was an interesting intercultural experience because the city is located where Germany, Belgium and the Netherlands meet. After six years there, I was hired at the University of Duisburg, which is also relatively close to the Dutch border.

It was in the late 80s and early 90s that I really got interested in looking at communication models, many influenced by American and British insights, but these models didn't fit in with my experiences. So I looked at the influence and impact of culture and more closely at intercultural communication. At the same time, I started working with Vincent Merk (former President of SIETAR Europa) and Jan Ulijn and others on a number of EU-sponsored projects. We were trying to bring intercultural and business elements to the teaching of English and German at Polish and Slovenian universities. In 1998, I was offered a professorship in business English and intercultural communication at Konstanz University of Applied Sciences.

You have spent most of your adult life in Germany. Would you say you have now gone "native"?

Many people ask me that. I say yes, and it's quite natural—German family, house in Germany, job for life in Germany. Some people who know me say I'm more German than British; then I say I'm 80% British and 60% German! They laugh but personal growth of that kind is a fantastic gift resulting from the intercultural experience. I've retained many British values while taking on German ones and, together, the whole is more than the sum of the parts. It's a mix of interlocking pieces.

Growing contact with the other culture means that you get insights into your values and norms, or at least become aware of them. Definitely a dual perspective, but it doesn't mean you lose the entirety of your culture of origin. When you're in Britain, you criticize the British and defend the Germans and when you're in Germany, you criticize the Germans and defend the British. The important thing is to be able to take on the other perspective, intellectually and emotionally.

In the book "Intercultural Interaction", you discuss how one becomes a qualified intercultural trainer. Could you say something about that?

Many students ask me, "How do I become an intercultural trainer?" I generally say, "Don't do it!" They have an academic background but no long-term experience of living in another culture, let alone the business world. A person needs to spend at least two or three years working abroad to gather the emotional experience of another cultural reality. This is a key point: for trainers to be credible, amongst other things they have to have genuine intercultural experience.

If you haven't worked abroad, you aren't taken seriously. And if you want to be an intercultural trainer in business, you need to have sound business and management experience. And not that of an intern. You actually need to be confronted with business and management realities which have serious consequences for you. And you need to have a few grey hairs… They help, too.

I do quite a lot of work for companies and organizations, where I meet people who are fully engaged in international management. The experiences I get there and the stories I'm told I take back into my teaching and research. It's a two-way cross-fertilization process. It's very important for my credibility at the university and in business to be able to have this dual view.

You also write in your book that schools can provide a better place for developing intercultural competence. Could you explain that?

You need to first ask yourself what does it take to be successful across cultures? And my answer is you need intercultural interaction competence. It's a multi-faceted phenomenon: the *right* knowledge, the *right* skills and the *right* attitudes and personal qualities. These are the three classical elements of intercultural development, repeatedly cited in publications.

Cultural knowledge, raising awareness of one's own culture, facts and figures, knowing and understanding—this is something that can be done in your classic two-day intercultural training. But skills need to be practiced. You can help people develop relationships, enlarge their repertoire of communication styles, talk about active listening but you need time to practice these things. And then you have attitudes and qualities: open-mindedness, flexibility, acceptance, taking the other perspective, nonjudgmentalness, for example. These are the sorts of things the trainer should be striving for and they can only be developed over time.

Interaction competence, if you look at its full scope, is something that can only be partially developed in short-term courses. And that's why school and university are better places to develop this competence. The students are there for longer and you can work on developing this competence over a longer time period. And this is where in the business setting in particular you need credibility, so you can make the case for long-term training. If you do a six-month program, it will be more effective and you'll have more sustainability. But it will be more difficult to sell

What are the biggest challenges in the intercultural profession?

I'm worried by the fact that anybody can do intercultural training, they just have to sell it to the client. The entry-barriers are minimal, a bit like the translation business—anybody can claim to be a translator. The client may not be in a position to judge quality. Very often, "quality" just means the customer is happy. That doesn't necessarily mean the trainer has done a good job.

Plus training has become a very desirable profession for a lot of young people who have spent a year abroad, done some intercultural courses at university, then an internship. I'm very uneasy about what this means for the profession. What you need is a set of standards. The profession, and SIETAR in particular, need to think about assessing the qualifications of a trainer. It would help not only the profession, but also help the client to know that they would get a minimum quality. The intercultural training profession could introduce a qualification assessment process. Trainers wouldn't necessarily need to have formal qualifications. They could get their experience recognized as being equivalent to a certain level of competence.

Another challenge is making new research available to trainers and developers. If you have up-to-date insights, it enhances your credibility as a trainer. We need a three-pronged approach involving the trainer, the researcher and business.

Let me explain by means of an example. An intercultural trainer is brought in to support a new international project. The trainer responds with a classic two-day course and the company is happy because they've done something. But the trainer could say, "In collaboration with researchers and academics, how about a longitudinal support-process? We won't just look at international teams generally; we'll also look at your team as it works over a period of time. Researchers will observe, interview and generate insights. Trainers will take these insights and develop modules—best practice for the people in this team and other teams." That's the value-added a company can get, a customized product.

There's a lot of research out there in business and international management. It seldom reaches the trainer. We need concerted cooperation to generate new insights. Researchers are not necessarily able to convince organizations they can help them. But if trainers show there's a real value-added, organizations might be more willing.

Can you give examples of research being used in training?

I headed a study for the European Commission on developing intercultural competence in the context of foreign language teaching in ten European countries. One of the interesting insights was that intercultural competence should be regarded as a transversal skill. In another words, it shouldn't just be taught in foreign language courses but also be an element in other subjects, across the curriculum. This has important implications. School teachers, who are handling some very complex situations, are now working with intercultural insights.

When I was appointed at Konstanz University, there was already an awareness that international communication was more than knowledge of the foreign language. My university established an innovative program called Asian Studies and Management, a combination of 50% language-culture-communication and 50% business administration. I was able to move into that program and help contribute to the research, development and teaching of intercultural management.

A very accessible and practical guide to intercultural communication.

What are you working on at the moment?

A new and expanded edition of *The Mindful International Manager* with Jeremy Comfort appeared at the beginning of 2014. A collection of case studies on intercultural management, edited together with Christoph Barmeyer and including cases by Nancy Adler, Fons Trompenaars as well as by well-known trainers. And another co-authored book, this time on culture and change management. I really like the close cooperation with a co-author which is involved in the joint creation of a satisfying text. So I have quite a bit on my plate for now and the next two years!

Interview with Robert Gibson

A passionate interculturalist in the business world

Back in the pioneer days of 2000, intercultural training was pretty straight-forward: you focused on the behavior patterns of a particular national culture. Increased sensitivity to foreign counterparts obviously leads to improved communication. But companies have now become more discriminating in their demands.

A new generation of managers, who have studied and worked abroad, are questioning the need for only intercultural training. The increasing diversity of projects depends on managers, engineers, sales reps and lawyers sharing knowledge and cooperating across different fields and cultures—intercultural sensitivity combined with leadership and management skills.

One person who has been at the forefront of adapting training to the contemporary needs of companies is Robert Gibson, senior consultant for intercultural business competence at Siemens AG in Munich. British by birth and education, he exemplifies the new breed: reflective, discreet, soft-spoken and highly articulate. The type who, while sizing up a situation, is already mapping out a strategy.

Active in the intercultural field for over 25 years, he was a founding member of SIETAR Deutschland as well as Vice-President of SIETAR Europa and remains an ardent spokesman. He also writes a popular column in the German magazine *Business Spotlight,* and is the author of the hands-on book *Intercultural Business Communication* (Oxford University Press). An expert "par excellence" on the emerging intercultural needs of the business world.

*Perhaps you can tell us about some of the experiences that led you toward becoming an intercul-
turalist in Germany...*

I grew up in Croydon, a suburb in South London—classic commuter-belt with a rail link
to the city. At school, I was very interested in history at an early age but a major event was
when I started learning German. I had an excellent teacher who got me really interested
in the language and it led to my first trip abroad, an exchange program in Hamburg when
I was 17.

After finishing school, I had a gap year before going off to study History and German at Oxford. I got a place in a program run by the *Deutsch-Britischer Jugendaustausch*
and lived in Berlin for six months in 1977. It was a fantastic opportunity to experience
the effects of world politics at first hand. I'd go cycling with my host family in Spandau
and suddenly we reached the Wall and couldn't go any further. But that didn't stop me
from getting to know people in East Berlin; I used to go there regularly, via Check-Point
Charlie or Friedrichstrasse.

In 1980, as a third-year student, I worked as an assistant at a teacher training college
in Vienna. Central and Eastern Europe was still blocked off and I travelled to places like
Prague and Budapest at weekends. At that time this was quite an adventure. I got to know
people there and conversations inevitably centred around our cultural differences.

After university I became a history teacher in Britain and, during summer holidays,
taught English in Poland and Hungary at summer camps run by UNESCO. I had a Polish
girlfriend, a significant person in my life, who was a leader of one of the camps. Our relationship made me realize how important cultural differences were.

How is it that you ended up in Germany?

In 1985 I received an offer to teach English and Cultural Studies at the University of
Munich. "Landeskunde" (geography, history, country's insitutions) was a rather dry
subject at the time and I looked for ways of making it more interesting and relevant for
the students. I discovered SIETAR, saw that there were professional interculturalists and
started going to their conferences and getting involved in the organization.

After five years at the university I was offered a position developing curricula for
vocational schools at the Bavarian Ministry of Education. This was an interesting experience and very good for my language skills because everything was in German and I had
to run workshops and meetings with teachers, business people and ministry officials.

This takes us to the topic of training teachers. As you have been through both the British and German systems, what differences do you see?

In Germany, I felt that a lot of effort was put into defining and developing a detailed curriculum; we had different courses for specific groups. For instance, I developed an English syllabus for opticians, based on the language an optician needs. In Britain it was the other way round at that time, not much emphasis on curriculum but much more on testing the pupils with standardized exams.

Some German students and teachers that I met were critical of the British school system; one even wrote an article about how British schools "wasted time" by keeping the pupils at school the whole day. I was brought up in Britain to see this as something positive, with much more emphasis on developing the whole personality of the pupil; we had clubs and activities in the lunch break and team sports after school This is where I saw a potential synergy effect: combining the holistic approach of the British with the German expertise in curriculum development and vocational education. I believe the two systems can still learn a lot from each other.

What did you do after your time at the Ministry of Education?

I spent eight years as Head of Business Languages at the School of Management of the University of Eichstätt-Ingolstadt. When I left school I thought the business world was the last place I wanted to work; I certainly didn't want to follow in the footsteps of my father who had worked as a chemical engineer for BP. But gradually I began to see that the interesting developments in the intercultural field were coming from business.

In 2000 there was a breakthrough: Siemens hired me to bring together their language and intercultural training programs. In moving from a university to a corporate environment, I had to make the case for intercultural training differently. It wasn't enough to say, "We have the best trainers, innovative methods and excellent materials." I had to show my clients how it helped them to be successful in their business The other things were of secondary importance. My mindset changed so much that, a few years later at a SIETAR conference, a colleague said, "Rob, you're talking different now!"

Your present role is to coordinate intercultural competence training at Siemens. What do you look for when hiring an interculturalist?

Siemens is a highly complex organization with cultures of different sectors and divisions, and products ranging from gas turbines for power stations to computer tomography machines for hospitals. Obviously building a power plant for a pulp factory in Finland is very different from dealing with hospital managers in China. We're looking for people who appreciate the complexity.

To be more precise, intercultural trainers need three qualities. One is relevant cultural knowledge and background. Clients often expect the trainer to come from the target culture. Trainers should work well in tandem, for example an expert from China working with a German facilitator.

The second is training skills and experience. This is probably the easiest quality to acquire if you have the right personality. We employ trainers for groups as well as expert coaches and consultants.

The third quality is often the hardest to find—appropriate business knowledge and experience. It is essential to link the intercultural content with the business at hand.

My advice to people studying intercultural communication who want jobs in the corporate world is to make sure you get as much business experience as possible through studies and internships. Intercultural training is not a stand-alone.

How do you decide if a person is qualified to facilitate training?

A trainer who comes with a ready-made product may not be so interesting to us. They might come with an excellent e-learning tool, but if it isn't compatible with our IT landscape then it is unlikely that we can work together. We are not just a broker of training but have our own distinct approach and develop our own materials in cooperation with external partners. I'd advise trainers to find out what companies are already doing and what they are really looking for rather than making too many assumptions.

I think that a very important quality in trainers is being "easy to do business with". Sometimes, a trainer will have a list of what equipment they want and we have to tell them, "Sorry, we can't do that. You will be doing this in a meeting room in a factory and they don't have the time to look for 4 flipcharts and 2 pin boards." We work under time pressure and do many different things, often at short notice. I don't always have time to discuss every detail with the trainer. It's all about being flexible without compromising on quality.

Another issue is respecting copyright. It's not enough to say I got the picture from the Internet. We need to know the source and be certain that we have the rights to use it. Otherwise, there might be compliance issues. As an individual, you can probably get away with it, but not as a company.

Are your clients satisfied with the intercultural training they receive?

We have a department dealing with intercultural competence and I still have a job so maybe that means yes. We are continually asking ourselves how to measure the effectiveness of training. Training is an investment and we have to provide reasons for people to put money into it.

One of my colleagues came up with the term "return on culture": investment in culture will pay off in business terms. Of course if we could demonstrate the return on culture, it would make training more appealing to our clients. "If you can't measure it, you can't manage it" is what people often say in the business world. I am not sure if you can really measure soft skills but believe that while the cultural factor is not measurable, it's perceivable. I'm increasingly finding clients who appreciate this and that culture can't be separated from a lot of other factors which play a role in their business. It's like salt in the soup; you can taste it but can't take it out.

On a more practical level, we have a standardized feedback process which is different from the "happy sheets" at the end of a seminar, where it might just be the participants' euphoria about a trainer's personality. What we do is send an email to all participants a week after the course and ask them to rate the workshop. After three months, they get another questionnaire asking them if they have applied what they learned and if not what the barriers were. We also compile investors' feedback by asking the person who paid for the training if they thought it was a good investment; they sometime have a different perspective from the participants.

Turning to another subject, what has it been like as a British national in Germany?

When I came to Germany all those years ago I didn't think there would be massive differences between Britain and Germany. There probably aren't in the world context. When you go to China, you expect people to be different. The differences between Britain and Germany are more subtle.

One of the main difference is in terms of communication style. Issues in Germany are often dealt with and understood in a very direct manner. For instance, the feedback I got after I ran a workshop was, "You use the word *vielleicht* (perhaps) too much." That made me think. The word suggested to my German colleague that I wasn't sure what I was doing. To me it was a way of trying not to be too bossy, softening the instructions to get the group on my side.

Or when a German says, "I gave a presentation in England and they said it was very interesting." I reply, "Oh dear." They are confused and then I point out that it may be that the British person was just being polite and didn't find it interesting at all. I like the saying "The Germans are too honest to be polite and the British are too polite to

Mr. Bean embodies the indirect communication style of the British, which sometimes confuses Germans.

be honest." After nearly 30 years in Germany, I have got used to this direct communication and even find it quite refreshing. I now get frustrated when I sense British people are beating around the bush. For many Germans, though, I'm still not direct enough.

Another area of difference is in the attitude to planning. This is connected to uncertainty avoidance. German colleagues often want a detailed agenda but I sometimes ask myself, why are we doing all this planning? I just feel like going in, doing something and seeing what happens. This can irritate them. For Germans planning provides security, a framework and a logical structure. The British tend to be more pragmatic, reacting to the situation rather than strictly following a plan The key to dealing with this is to be aware of the differences.

For me, the challenge is to combine empathy with being authentic. Even after such a long time in Germany I still discover new differences. I think that your cultural identity is probably formed in your childhood but I have changed a bit. Maybe I'm now somewhere in the middle of the North Sea. Living in another culture, you discover a lot about where you come from. When I was at Munich University, students would ask, "Why do you have a monarchy in Britain?" Although I'd studied history, I couldn't come up with an answer.

Finally, could you tell us how you became involved with SIETAR?

SIETAR has been very important for my development. The first contact I had with the organization was a wonderful SIETAR International conference in Kilkenny, Ireland in 1990. What struck me was the diversity of the people I met—not only their national cultures, but also their professional ones. Next to me at dinner the first day was somebody from the U.S. Peace Corps in jeans and a manager from the World Bank in a smart business suit. The exchange of ideas was fascinating.

At that time SIETAR International was very active in the U.S. and many members were Americans living abroad. We wanted to have more conferences in Europe so the idea of SIETAR Europa was born. A fews years later people then said we should found SIETAR at another level in Germany and I hosted the first SIETAR Deutschland conference in Ingolstadt in 1994. I was able to offer use of the seminar rooms at my university. I recall saying, "The great thing is we don't have any real costs. We buy a bottle of whisky for the caretaker and pay someone to clean up at the end. If we have 10 people, that's okay, if we have 200 people, that's okay." In fact we had about 130 people.

Today, both SIETAR Europa and SIETAR Deutschland have become much more professional. I really enjoy going to the regional meetings here in Munich. Someone gives a talk or a workshop and people meet and share experiences. "By members, for members"—I think it's a great model.

What we need for the future is a combination of these two things: active regional and national SIETARs, but also a body like SIETAR Europa to bring everyone together, including people who don't have a national organization of their own. The key is that the combination of cultural and functional diversity be retained. It would be sad if it became an organization just for trainers or just for researchers. SIETAR's uniqueness is that it brings together interculturalists from different national and professional cultures.

I'm most grateful for the experience I had on the international Board as well as the workshops and conferences I've attended. It's played a major role in my development. To begin with I asked myself why I was spending so much time and money going to meetings. Looking back, it was one of the best investments I have ever made.

My advice to people would be to get involved with SIETAR. You may have very idealistic visions of what you want to do, but also be prepared to do practical things. And you really meet some fantastic people. SIETAR is a great network.

Interview with Sylvia Schroll-Machl

Fostering cultural cohesion

As its citizens are proud to tell you, Bavaria is a "free state", one of the oldest in Europe, and "Bavarians first, Germans second" describes the sentiment. However this once rural kingdom has transformed itself into one of Germany's most dynamic high-tech centers, making it a curious combination of "laptops and Lederhosen."

The need to be different—and apart—goes back millennia; a Roman writer called the Bavarians "a stubborn mountain folk", a portrait expounded on by Johann Wolfgang von Goethe. That stubbornness has generated a strong creative pulse, perhaps best exemplified by King Ludwig II, the reclusive and eccentric monarch who provided the world with the splendid, fairy-tale Neuschwanstein castle. Ludwig was also one of the first who saw Richard Wagner's genius, supporting him lavishly and sponsoring Bayreuth's Festspielhaus. For music lovers, Bavaria remains the land of Wagner.

The Bavarian attitude is still alive and kicking today and a good example is Dr. Sylvia Schroll-Machl, one of the most original thinkers to have come onto the intercultural scene in years. Born and raised in Lower Bavaria, she went on to study religion, history and psychology in Munich and Regensburg.

Her widely-acclaimed book *Die Deutschen — Wir Deutsche* (published in English as *Doing Business with Germans — Their Perception, Our Perception*) is an audacious attempt to understand the German mindset. Deeply intuitive, but strictly adhering to empirical research, she amazes the reader by really explaining what it means to be German. Her direct, personal style makes for a book that's different from anything you have ever read. Her intercultural training sessions are like that too—very personal and authentically German.

Perhaps you can start by talking about the turning points in your life that led you to become an interculturalist.

I was born in Deggendorf and have lived here all my life; my family has been here since the early 1600s, which makes me very proud. I feel attached to my town and comfortable with my surroundings. For this reason, when I list the five things that led me to become an interculturalist, my upbringing takes on the least importance.

Nonetheless, during my youth, my family and I visited relatives in the former German Democratic Republic every year. And because Deggendorf is near the Czech border,

Growing up next to the Czech border made Sylvia Schroll-Machl curious about how other people live.

I developed a relationship with being on the periphery, curious and fascinated about who lived on the other side.

When the Wall fell in 1989, it was a liberation for me: finally I could get to know these people! This is when I started to do a large research project on cultural comparisons in post-communist countries at the Economic University of Vienna.

The second factor is that I'm deeply Christian, which means I have a strong wish to do something worthwhile in life.

After my *Abitur,* I studied Catholic theology in Munich, then began work as a counselor in a Catholic youth center in Passau. I was very involved with the German-Israeli youth exchange and visited Israel several times. I now realize my theological studies not only helped me understand my own culture, but allowed me access to other cultures in a beautiful way. For example, when I tell people of the Muslim faith that I'm a Catholic theologian, their respect for me increases enormously. This is because their culture teaches them that any religious person is a decent person.

The third factor is my tremendous interest in psychology. Issues like managing intergroup relations or how values, standards and norms come into being fascinate me. They go with my philosophy of trying to understand people, how to get access to a person. I thought it would be fascinating to do basic research in the social-psychological aspects that make people tick. Psychology represents no great ideology and allows you to live with the principles of humanism. So after six years of working with young people, I went back to study psychology, and later specialized with Professor Alexander Thomas at the University of Regensburg.

Now, if I were to arrange the pillars in the order that led to my profession, first would be psychology, second religion, and third Alexander Thomas, a great and lovable man, a human being. Although I did parallel work in clinical psychology and passed my exams to become a psychotherapist, I chose to go the route of intercultural psychology because of Professor Thomas. He introduced me to the research of cultural standards theory, which I did my dissertation on. It's about perception, thinking, values, actions, a typology which means so much to me. Everything that I've done up to now revolves almost exclusively around the cultural standard approach.

I've observed how often these cultural standards as well as Thomas are unfairly criticized. I think it is everyone's right to make critical points but many of those who criticize don't possess the background in psychology necessary to understand the concepts. Furthermore, I believe it is counterproductive to play one intercultural approach against another and to make an ideology out of it. Each one has his or her epistemological and legitimate approach with its strengths and weaknesses. Everyone is struggling to generate the best possible work. It hurts me to read again and again the prejudices others have against "culture standards". All models have advantages and disadvantages.

The fourth pillar was my husband, Reinhold. When I finished studies in intercultural communications in 1992, there was no general awareness of the field, let alone the importance of training. So, when I went for a job interview at companies like BMW, they would say "intercultural what?"

Although I knew my subject well, I wasn't at all skilled at persuading companies of its importance. So my husband, also a psychologist in therapeutic practice, said, "If you can't find a permanent position, why don't you become freelance? I'll sponsor you." That's how I launched my career.

My husband, who has since passed away, took care of everything, the home, garden and household, so that I could devote myself fully to my profession. It took almost three years until I began to earn a living. I am very grateful to him. Without his support my career would have never taken off. But looking back now, this difficult time had less to do with my inexperience than the fact that the field of intercultural training was in its pioneer period.

When I speak to you or read your books and articles, you somehow perfectly incarnate the German soul. Could you explain how you do this so well?

Here, I have to say two things. First, I feel very "rooted" in my Bavarian and German culture, which allows me to be acutely aware of the German reality. My German customers who have not lived abroad and have to be sensitive to international markets feel

I understand them. And if I do a Germany seminar for non-Germans, I always get feed-back about being "authentic" and witty. This is what I call positive self-confidence and it's important for intercultural competence. It includes learning to be alone and being satisfied with yourself, your roots.

Second, my love for cultural and historical references is based on my studies of history and religion, which are important in understanding mentality imprinting. When long historic causes are explained, people feel they understand others better. They realize that a value that's 500 years old won't change in two months and this makes them open to other solutions. Participants often say, "Our foreign partners have to see our way." I answer, "Your partners have been using this method for 500 years and they think their way's okay." It's then they say, "Oh yeah, you're right."

Are there other aspects of your training that make your seminars so popular?

Well, in every seminar, I try to do a lot of coaching. That is, work with the issues and questions of the participants, and that's when I really feel I'm in my element. My training as a psychologist comes into play, I ask in what kind of situations they have difficulties, where they have inhibitions, when they're uncomfortable. I then ask them to explain the reasons why in detail and have them adapt their behavior accordingly. That's what I love to do and I have the feeling that people appreciate it.

For example, I had a seminar recently where I had a couple of people adjust their role-play so they could appreciate the German way better. The participants were deeply moved by this mind-shifting and said, "My God, I understand them now."

I've always felt that people benefit from this sort of coaching and also feel more comfortable. It's the sort of learning that doesn't go through the head but through the heart. This is far more effective than having participants do a couple of games, which only leads to a small transfer.

Are there situations that you find difficult in training?

Yes, ethical issues. I should point out that in 80% of the seminars I conduct, there are no ethical problems; it's just those other 20% related to globalization that put me in an awkward position. I can't ignore the fact that we are living in a globalized word. On one hand, it's beautiful; on the other hand, parts of it can be cruel.

This is where dilemmas present themselves: bribery, discrimination, wage-dumping, prostitution, human rights violations. Take child labor. People say, "The state must make sure that children don't work" but when subcontractors use child labor, we look the other way and pay for the goods. I often sit and think to myself, "Careful, careful, Sylvia, you wanted to do something meaningful in your life. What are you supporting now?"

I often can sense when a person who is being forced by management to do something unethical and is telling me indirectly: "How can I look at myself in the mirror?" I'm ready to talk with those people, acknowledge their feelings, and encourage them to give critical feedback to top management. However, sometimes I sense the person sitting in front of me wants to learn tricks to exploit counterparts in an elegant intercultural way—or be involved in a process of transferring jobs abroad, whereby the local people have to give away their know-how to others, which eventually leads to their unemployment. Then I must always ask myself: "How is the dignity of these people maintained? How is the local management dealing with these people?"

Does it work?

Sometimes yes, sometimes no. And if not, I try to help people to think about and question unethical practices. Sometimes I get into trouble with the client. But if a seminar is to be fruitful for both sides, it must be based on mutual respect. This is the principle in my seminars, to create esteem not only for other cultures but also for oneself.

There are, of course, companies that have developed good guidelines regarding the moral dilemmas. I find this to be more often the case with mid-size companies than your large corporations, which are more anonymous. And when I read the literature and intercultural management concepts, I often have the feeling that it doesn't at all reflect ethical behavior. Don't get me wrong, I'm not against globalization, I see and understand the problems. But there are times when I say to management, "Wait a minute here. I'm not sure this is the right way."

In your book "Die Deutschen — Wir Deutsche", you point out the cultural standard of separation of personal and public domain. Everyone in the world makes this distinction but it seems Germany is where it's carried to the extreme, resulting in Germans being seen as too formal and serious. Could you give the historical reasons why this is so?

This separation of the personal and public domains, I would think, is due to two historical events. First, in the centuries of German territorial fragmentation, restrictions and confinement were everyday experiences. Boundaries of daily reality increasingly became "boundaries of the mind" as well. By the middle of the 18th century, there were approximately 1600 different territories on German soil, and even at the beginning of the 19th century some 1000 still existed, the boundaries of which could not be easily crossed.

Die Deutschen — Wir Deutsche (English edition)

Additionally, the separation of internal and external areas provided important protection against falling into the clutches of the reigning absolute ruler. People learned to lead a confined life-style in a small circle of close friends as a natural reaction to the adverse political circumstances.

The second point to remember is the teachings of Martin Luther. He preached that the church needed to remove emotional and irrational elements from religious ceremonies — feelings were not a necessary part of faith. An intellectual, rational connection to God was far more solid. And, if you look closely, Protestantism lacks a cultish aspect in the form of worship or spiritual sacrifice. As a result people related less passionately to religion and became more intellectual. Catholicism is simply more emotional, exemplified by festivals, processions, theater, carnival.

Over generations, the Protestant approach led to a clear emphasis on objectivity and rationality. In fact, you could say modern Germany was largely moulded by Protestant theology. Furthermore, the Lutheran faith emphasizes a separation of life-spheres, which eventually led to task-orientation (concentration on the task at hand) and toward a richness of spirit (the individual inner life).

Then why don't Lutheran countries such as Sweden, Norway and Denmark make a strong distinction between public and private?

Because they didn't suffer from all the wars. Germany has the misfortune of being *das Land der Mitte;* pan-European conflicts often took place on German territory, such as the Thirty Years War, followed by many others and ending with WWII. The separation between public and private can be seen as a protective mechanism.

After WWII, Germans had to learn how to deal with their feelings of sorrow, guilt and disaster and they did this by separating their feelings from the awful reality. Otherwise, they would have all had to commit collective suicide. Redemption was found in perfectionist behavior, absolute correctness to counteract their feelings of worthlessness in an environment of total chaos.

Another point to consider is the relative lack of social mobility of Germans. During the lengthy period in which small German states predominated, citizens had a stable social fabric and relative immobility. It also implied relationships didn't have to be re-negotiated. Consequently, it was much easier to concentrate on common objectives or tasks.

Take me, I know all the people in my town from birth, I don't need to develop behavior for contact with strangers. This is different from people in Holland or the city-state Hamburg. Their commercial tradition forced them to talk to foreigners. Something quite different from a town in Bavaria or Baden-Württemburg where you almost always found your relationships in the local tavern.

What I have just told you is known as the history of mentalities, generated from historical research. It's based on extreme hypothetical thinking that seems very logical and consistent but that doesn't necessarily mean it's the absolute truth. If a real historian were to question me, he could tear my points apart. What I want to say is that they are meaningful and useful and we use them to help people in accepting cultural differences more easily.

Martin Luther, painted in 1528 by Lucas Cranach the Elder

Fascinating. Now, to end this interview, what would be your advice for a successful international cooperation?

You need to, above all, accept diversity and work with it. Of course, there's no "one and only" strategy for handling all international cooperation—the appropriate strategy depends mainly upon three factors, what I describe as a triangle. First there's the situation, that is the task at hand or the context of the intercultural interaction. Then there's the people involved and lastly their culture. Furthermore, if an intercultural exchange is to be fruitful for both sides, it must be based on mutual respect, even—and especially—when the other person does not live up to our own expectations and values.

In my seminars, I always strive to supply the participants with the tools for understanding why Germans behave the way they do, but also to give them an insight into how this is seen by an outsider to the culture, whose definition of what is normal and expected behavior is different. The easiest response to intercultural misunderstandings is avoidance; the most dangerous is to dominate the intercultural situation through, for example, economic power. The most challenging is to understand the differences and their causes. Without a doubt, this last option is slow, strenuous and difficult. But it is the only one that guarantees continuous, mutually satisfying relations between citizens of different nations.

Non-conventional truths
about American–German partnerships

In 1995, German psychologist Sylvia Schroll-Machl examined the reasons American-German projects often fail. A German multinational brought her in to evaluate how American and German engineers and researchers interacted. It became clear early on that problems were due, in large part, to misunderstanding each other's way of problem-solving.

Schroll-Machl noticed that, at the outset of a project, Germans showed a greater need for detailed information and discussion. They tended to see the process from an engineering point of view, considering all of the difficulties that might arise, planning hypothetical solutions. The goal was to make sure everything would be done correctly, every element possible kept "under control". Avoiding uncertainty means avoiding anxiety.

During the initial discussion-phase, the Germans expected all team members to share knowledge by sketching out their previous experiences. Reaching a consensus (which, they argued, permits the rapid implementation of any strategy) was essential. *Schroll-Machl concluded that German decision-making concentrated on identifying problems, their history and components. Less emphasis was placed on results.*

The action-oriented Americans found these discussions trying, often outright boring. The exchange of too much information felt like a waste of time, "paralysis through analysis". No matter how good a plan is, the thinking goes, it will be modified along the way. The Americans didn't speak up at this stage; by not saying anything, they hoped to speed up the process and get down to work. In their minds, problem-solving started out with a short brainstorming session to define goals and establish a series of approximate milestones.

Efficiency and creativity were the watchwords. The Americans wanted to "keep all options open", perceiving any project as a trial-and-error process. *Schroll-Machl found their decision-making to be more open-ended, concentrating on a mission, a vision.*

The Germans felt that with this approach, the Americans were acting without understanding the problem: a cowboy mentality of shooting first and asking questions later." On the other hand, the Americans felt obsession with plans, and sticking to them, meant being locked into a rigid pattern, with no flexibility during the implementation-phase.

Once a plan was established, German team members were able to work relatively independently. Americans expected further group meetings and informal communication throughout. The Germans complained that the Americans asked about issues which had already been discussed at length.

Basic philosophies—"going on a mission" vs "minding the shop"—were only part of the equation, though. Americans are often given tasks for which they have not been thoroughly trained. Frequent job-rotation leads to a "learn-by-doing" attitude. With this attitude, they automatically communicate more with superiors, as well as other team members. Germans are, on the whole, better trained. Mechanics, machinists and the like go through the famous *Dualsystem* but even engineers and executives receive a holistic mix of the practical and the theoretical. And, of course, the rules for doing business in Germany are stricter: whether it's cars, cosmetics or cold cuts, there are norms, guidelines, documentation which one actually has to read.

Germans also assume decisions made at group meetings are binding. Americans see them as guidelines which change when the need arises or a better solution presents itself. And Americans expect these changes to take place; it's part of the adventure!

Lastly, because Americans instinctively emphasize the relationship side when communicating, they have a tendency to share more of their personality with co-workers. Germans, who by nature wish to remain credible and objective when communicating, tend to maintain a more impersonal "work only" relationship with colleagues. This explains, in large part, why Americans complain that Germans don't seem to be very open in conversing about a project during the implementation phase.

It is interesting that the nationality of the leader generated different internal dynamics. If the leader is German, the group is more like a coalition. The leader is both an expert and a mediator (expected to convince, not order) who tends to vote with the group. During the implementation phase, there's little interaction with individual group members. "Distant" and "difficult to reach out to" was the way the Americans put it. The American leader defines goals, makes decisions, distributes tasks and makes sure they're done. Motivation and coaching are part of the chain-of-command style.

Schroll-Machl's study makes clear that if these differences are explained at the beginning, i.e. through intercultural training, chances for success increase enormously. However, if cultural awareness is not made a priority and the different communication styles are not understood, German-American projects often fail, causing both financial loss and hurt feelings.

A different view
on the German "export machine"

A few years ago (2011), I received a telephone call from a Polish journalist, who wanted to know why it was that Germany, despite heavy economic losses in the 2008 recession, was currently experiencing a second *Wirtschaftswunder.* He noted that with an economy expanding by an amazing 3.6% last year, Germany was leaving the other advanced economies in the dust.

If you talk to experts, Germany's star performance is due in large part to its "export machine", shipping more goods per capita than any other country in the world. For over a century, it has built a reputation of making products second to none in precision, reliability and quality. And despite high wage costs and relatively expensive prices, it seems that the world can't get enough of "Made in Germany" products.

Was it the famous *Mittelstandbetriebe,* the mid-size companies that made Germany such a powerful exporter, the journalist asked? That's one way of viewing it, I said. I pointed out that many of Germany's top exporters come from Baden-Württemberg, which was historically Germany's poorest agricultural region. The 19ᵗʰ century was exceptionally severe, compelling many to tinker and invent to survive.

That environment generated people like Gottlieb Daimler, inventor of the first automobile, and Robert Bosch, creator of the electric engine. They were diligent—never doing something half-way, as well as thinkers—always trying to improve on everything in existence.

The famous Daimler star well symbolizes Germany's mastery (and need) of precision.

Their inventions led to the founding of many successful companies, both mid-size and large, and their spirit of tinkering remains important today.

Yet, to really understand why mid-size companies generally do better in Germany than in other countries, one has to consider the German mindset, the cognitive ways Germans organize everyday actions and thoughts.

Much of what we now call "typically German" (diligence, perfection, need for order) can be attributed to a relatively dreadful past. As any psychologist will tell you, a traumatized child often becomes a perfectionist as an adult. Germany has suffered more than its share of horror, beginning with the Thirty Years War (1618–1648). It had the misfortune of being *das Land der Mitte,* the country in the middle, in a religious conflict involving Sweden, Denmark, France, Spain and Austria. Over seven million Germans died in less than two generations, 35% of the population. The psycho-social toll the Germans suffered would have a profound impact for centuries to come.

And other tragedies were to follow: the Napoleonic Wars, the Austro-Prussian War and, finally, two World Wars in the space of… 30 years. In the last of these, the Holocaust, brought disgrace and shame upon the German people as a whole.

Given Germany's tragic and violent past, it's not surprising that these wars have resulted in a survival strategy based on *Angst* about any form of uncertainty, a need for security. *Ordnung muß sein.* Order must reign.

Foreigners who arrive in Germany for the first time are surprised by the national need to do everything correctly; planning is essential and almost nothing is improvised. When German companies export, they want to make sure that everything is done right, including intercultural communication. It's no accident that the largest national SIETAR organization in the world happens to be in Germany.

This need for order is reflected on German TV. The country's highest-rated television program for the past 50 years is, in fact, *die Tagesschau,* the evening news. Not surprisingly, the host speaks in a monotone voice and emotion is taboo. Whatever is happening in the world, things aren't out of control.

Even simple gestures, like paying at the supermarket, are revealing. German customers normally have their money out before the cashier announces the total. Individuals subordinate their actions to the collective need to do things efficiently.

This sense of efficient planning is instilled at an early age. An American colleague who lives in Munich once told me about the time her twelve-year-old son broke his arm and had to miss a few days of school. Upon returning, he was quizzed on the Latin verbs his classmates had studied while he was gone. He said he'd been in the hospital but the teacher told him it was no excuse and failed him.

The boy's German father said, "you've learned a good lesson." His American mother, on the other hand, was up in arms and went to see the teacher. She was told not to worry, her son wouldn't fail the class, but it was made clear to her that this sort of learning experience laid the seeds for responsible behavior.

Need for order and abhorrence of uncertainty imply efficient collective behavior. *Machen wir es richtig!* Let's do it right! Once a decision is made or a project started, Germans subconsciously coordinate their own ideas and efforts toward group success. They know the sum is often far greater than the parts.

The German preposition *mit* (with) is used in countless expressions involving teamwork—*mitmachen, Mitarbeiter, Mitbestimmung*—and shows a spirit of togetherness which permeates all levels of society.

"Mitmachen" (doing something together) is a very important leitmotif among Germans.

This cooperative spirit is also found in the often heard phrase *Wir müssen höchste Leistung bringen,* which has no real equivalent in English. Literally, it means "we must bring about the highest output or peformance", but it is often translated as "we must work very intensively". The *Autobahn,* where driving at top speeds is often the norm, is a metaphor of this German collective need for high performance and passionate intensity.

These were my immediate impressions when I first began working in Germany over 30 years ago. A few years later I was listening to Richard Wagner's *Tannhäuser* at the *Stuttgarter Opernhaus* and couldn't help but associate collective strength with the overture. It is a haunting music which seems to capture the quintessence of the German soul, a passion to be earnest and dedicated to the common good.

As *Time Magazine* once noted, Germans are brilliant organizers and planners who like complexity and are good at integrating things, including people, into a big system. When 80 million people share that mindset on a daily basis, it makes for a powerful competitive advantage in the world marketplace.

Empathy and wealth

The concept of empathy is inseparable from intercultural sensitivity. The premise of any training is that a feeling of compassion needs to be developed, which in turn leads to better communication. Empathy, however, is not equally distributed and this has major implications in intercultural relations. Essentially, research has shown that one's sense of wealth vis-a-vis others determines to what degree he or she is willing to enter into another person's subjective world.

In its April, 2012 issue, *Scientific American* published a fascinating article. *How Wealth Reduces Compassion* reviews the latest studies on the relationship between empathy and material wealth and comes to the conclusion that the richer you are, the less likely you are to act fairly.

On first reflection, this would seem to go against common sense. If you already have enough to take care of yourself and your family, wouldn't you be inclined to think about others' needs? Not according to Berkeley psychologists Paul Piff and Dacher Keltner.

They conducted experiments on whether social class (education, wealth, job prestige) influences how much we care about the feelings of others. In one study, they surveyed drivers at a busy four-way intersection. Drivers of luxury cars were found to be more likely to cut off other drivers rather than wait their turn. Upper-class drivers also tended not to stop for a person trying to cross the street, even after making eye contact.

Later, Piff and his colleagues came up with a clever approach as to whether selfishness leads to wealth (rather than vice-versa). Participants were asked to compare themselves to people better or worse off than themselves. Before leaving, they were shown a jar of candy and told they could take home as much as they wished, what was left would be given to children in a room close by. The participants who thought of themselves as better off took far more, leaving little behind for the children.

Another study examined how social class influences compassion. On a regular basis, less affluent people were more likely to describe feelings of compassion for people who were said to be suffering. Results were unchanged after controlling for factors such as gender, ethnicity and spiritual beliefs.

Similarly, participants from different social classes watched a video about children with cancer and their hearts were monitored. Those on the lower end of the spectrum (for both income and education) were more likely to display compassion and their heart rates slowed down considerably—they were paying more attention to what they were seeing and hearing.

Other research tells us that the higher the social strata, the less likely people are to recognize the emotions of others. They also pay less attention to those with whom they interact, simultaneously doodling or checking email on their smart phones.

The intriguing question is why research consistently shows that wealth and status decrease our feelings of empathy? Conversely, if you have fewer resources, wouldn't you be more likely to be selfish? Piff suspects this paradox is related to the feelings that abundance gives us, a sense of self-importance and relative independence. The less we depend on others, the less we may care about their feelings.

And then there's the new attitude we have toward wealth, as depicted in the films *Wall Street* and *The Wolf of Wall Street*. Beginning in the 1980s, financiers and entrepreneurs began championing the mantra, "Greed is good". Thirty-five years later the gap between rich and poor in Western democracies has returned to what it was in 1929, on the eve of the Great Depression.

As anyone who reads a newspaper knows, the Crash of 2008 changed nothing except to transfer trillions of taxpayers' dollars across the developed world from public coffers to private industry and bank vaults. Most of the same people continue to run the finance and business sectors, doing business the same way, paying themselves the same bonuses. And right-wing politicians the world over continue to fight against regulation of any sort.

If we accept the research-based premise that social class influences empathy, it stands to reason that people of privilege are the least likely to make decisions that help those in need. Yet political power has always resided among the upper classes and—with increased deregulation of campaign financing—this has never been more true than today.

The u.s. Presidential election of 2012 may well give us a peek at the future. Republican candidate Mitt Romney bragged about forcing welfare mothers to work when he was governor of Massachusetts. He earned over $21 million dollars in 2010 without having to work himself, a simple return on his investments. He paid only 13.9% in income tax (far less than most American workers) but wanted to cut taxes even further, as well as many of the social programs they pay for. And although he got rich by closing companies and out-sourcing labor to China, India and Mexico, he said he had no need to apologize for success in business. During the campaign, when asked about students who couldn't afford to go to college, he suggested all they had to do was borrow the money from their parents.

The most disturbing thing of all is that he almost won the election.

Intercultural bloopers

Marketing people are by nature creative, always looking for ways to attract the attention of potential customers. And when a marketing campaign is successful, manufacturers immediately want to export it to other countries. Unfortunately, the literal translation of an ad can sometimes lead to serious intercultural misunderstandings, as the following examples make clear.

Kentucky Fried Chicken
When American fast food giant Kentucky Fried Chicken opened their first restaurant in Beijing in 1987, they accidentally mistranslated KFC's famous slogan, "Finger-lickin' good" to "We'll Eat Your Fingers Off!" in Chinese.

Texican Whopper
When this ad was published in Spain, the ambassador of Mexico in Spain issued a formal protest to Burger King and asked the company to pull the ad as well as apologize for offending Mexican cuisine. The poster shows a short wrestler wearing the Mexican flag as a cloak (disrespect to the Mexican flag is considered an offense in Mexico). And the Texican is described "the taste of Texas with a little spicy Mexican".

Big Mac
The Big Mac was originally sold in France under the name *Gros Mec*. In French, that translates as "big pimp".

Pepsi
When Pepsi started marketing its products in China a few years back, they translated their slogan, "Pepsi Brings You Back to Life" pretty literally. The slogan in Chinese really meant, "Pepsi Brings Your Ancestors Back from the Grave."

"Got Milk" Campaign

In the early 1990s the California milk industry's increasing concerns with sinking sales lead them to launch a new publicity campaign. They created the slogan "got milk" and it became the most successful campaign ever. But in Spanish-speaking populations it had no success whatsoever. Translated into Spanish the slogan sounds like "¿Tienes leche?"—meaning "are you giving milk?"

Clairol

The hair product company Clairol launched a curling iron called "Mist Stick" in Germany. *Mist* in German is slang for manure. It turns out manure sticks aren't very popular in Germany.

Parker Pen

Parker Pen's famous slogan "It won't leak in your pocket and embarrass you" was translated into Spanish and confused many Mexican consumers who read it as, "It won't leak in your pocket and make you pregnant."

Mont Blanc & Gandhi

Not only was Gandhi opposed to the British colonial rule, but he believed in frugality. Well-educated upwardly mobile Indians, the target market for luxury brands, may be attracted to luxury but were not pleased with the ad from Mont Blanc, as it associated the expensive pen with the ascetic Indian leader.

Nokia

In 2011, the mobile phone manufacturer Nokia, released the "Lumia" smartphone with great success, particularly when competing against Samsung and Apple. However, they neglected to check what *lumia* means in Spanish… turns out it means "prostitute".

Benetton

Benetton's advertising campaign was meant to provoke and it played with cultural taboos. Their campaign brought them attention, prizes and controversy. In Poland, however, with a conservative Catholic population, no motif could create more resentment than a picture of a priest kissing a nun.

Chevy Nova

In 1962 Chevrolet launched a complete-ly new car on the market, the Nova. Unexpectedly, in Spanish speaking countries the model sold badly. Nova sounds in Spanish like *no va:* as "no go". No wonder the customers were skepti-cal. Several years later, the Novas were manufactured in Argentina — and sold under the name "Chevy Special".

Mazda Laputa

The Mazda Laputa is a car from Mazda in Japan. The Laputa was introduced in 1999 as a sort of SUV/compact car mix. The name turned out to be unfit for Portuguese and Spanish-speaking countries, since "la puta" in Spanish means literally "the whore."

EXAMINING THE DANCE

Slipping in and out of cultures

The interculturally competent person

How do we recognize the beginnings of intercultural competence? A good place to start is complex allegiance, where a person's identity becomes less fixed. Thoughts and emotions are less a product of previous beliefs than an on-going process of understanding. Sense of self moves in and out of different subjective worldviews; one no longer thinks in ethnocentric terms but according to ambiguous conditions, a natural juggling of value-systems.

The essay on Arnold Schwarzenegger is an excellent example of what I call "bicultural belonging". When visiting *die Heimat,* he's as Austrian as it gets. But when he returns to California, he's home...

A truly intercultural person speaks more than one language and knows that language is far more than a means of communication—not so much a system of vocabulary, grammar and syntax as a shared perception of the world. Experience and meaning are connected via a shared framework and each new linguistic reality teaches you more about yourself.

The intercultural person is able to see and feel the relativity of beliefs, of decisions: an "absolute standard of rightness" no longer exists. Instead the process is dynamic, a continuing awareness of your own cultural boundaries. Which, in turn, allows you to expand your own parameters and wander into another person's mind.

Take the well-adjusted Brazilian manager of a Brazilian-German pharmaceutical company outside of Frankfurt. He wants to develop a new marketing campaign on a trial-and-error basis but knows his team will feel insecure about it. Understanding that the German need to plan things out is real, not frivolous, he comes up with a reassuring analogy. "It's not a hit-or-miss operation, quite the contrary. What we're doing is running a loop in a flow-chart on daily sales and will adapt the campaign accordingly."

Marco Polo was willing to open up to other cultures and accept different ways of living, as depicted in this 18th-century print, showing him in a Tatar costume.

This "other" perspective builds on empathy and permits events to be reconstructed as alternative cultural experiences. However, the ability to see oneself according to dual frames of reference—a sort of "dynamic in-between-ness"—can cause some to lose their primary cultural identity and create what might be described as internal culture shock.

The breakdown of identity leads to cultural marginality, an existence on the periphery of two (or more) cultures. Milan Kundera's "unbearable lightness of being" takes on real meaning here. If each life is ultimately insignificant, the decisions you make, whether based on your own culture or an adopted one, don't matter: they have no weight, they don't tie you down.

But insignificance is unbearable. When our decisions lose their importance, our lives are set adrift. We no longer exist as clearly defined individuals. It's a common condition among long-term expatriates and "global nomads." Conflicting identities often lead them to seek out other cultural marginals rather than people belonging to a specific group.

Despite periodic identity-confusion and the "unbearable lightness" of an uprooted life, such people may find roles as global mediators. The attempt to understand and reconcile cultural differences in both perception and expression is a worthy personal goal as well as a viable career opportunity.

In any case, one's true values are never at risk—a degree of ethnocentrism remains in fundamental habits of mind, which co-exist with "other-culture awareness." Every person needs a healthy identity-based ego and tested approaches to life.

We are, however, being forced to move from a "nationalistic worldview" to the universal recognition that each culture is unique and must be accepted for what it is before any real communication is possible.

The charming Austrians

A story of style in communicating

The majority of non-German tourists who come to Austria assume that the country is like Germany because Austrians speak German. And a quick look at their history tells us of an intertwining relationship to their northern neighbor. Austria suffered during World War II and all the other wars in which Germany was involved. One would think sharing a common historical fate, along with the same language and many similar cultural values, Austrians would have the same communication style.

Yet, Germans will quickly tell you that this isn't the case at all. For them, Austrians seem to be unclear, "wishy-washy", when they communicate. You can note this in the language. When a German says he'll do something, he'll say *Wir machen es.* You get a clear sense that the task will be done. An Austrian is more likely to say *Wir machen es schon.* The underlying message is we will try to get it done.

Or take the Austrian concept of promise—*versprechen.* I learned it within a few days after moving to Vienna. After my wife and I finished unpacking, we had a lot of cardboard boxes that belonged to the moving company. I called up and was told by a nice, young woman that a truck would come by on Friday. All I had to do was put the boxes out on the sidewalk, which I did. But by Friday late afternoon, they were still there. I called the company and before I could say a word about this unpleasant situation, the young lady immediately apologized and promised me in a most charming manner the boxes would be picked up the next day. Her seductive charm melted away a potential conflict.

So I brought all the boxes back into the apartment and, the next day, dragged them all back out to the sidewalk. I assumed that a promise meant a promise, the way I experienced it in Germany. No, the boxes weren't picked up on Saturday. There were finally taken away on Tuesday!

Interculturalist Frank Brück writes in his book *Interkulturelles Management: Kultur Vergleich Österrreich, Deutschland, Schweiz,* "Whereas Germans like to be objective, direct and credible, Austrians emphasize relationships and avoid conflict." And as one young Viennese summed it up to me, *Die Österreicher sind ein fröhliches Volk,* (the Austrians are a happy people) always trying to smile and maintain *Gemütlichkeit* (cosiness) with others, even if it means not doing what they say they're going to do.

Why do Austrians have such different communication strategies than the Germans? I've been observing how they communicate and also done some reading. These three historical points may provide an explanation.

The influence of Catholicism

Austria is a Catholic culture. Catholicism is a religion of synthesis, acting as a mediator between Man and God. It teaches sins can be forgiven through the act of confession. Psychologically, this has an enormously liberating effect—the heavy burden of self-responsibility is gone. Light-hearted behavior is possible; sins can be washed clean; nothing is starkly black and white...

Not so in Germany, heavily influenced by the writings of Luther and Calvin. It teaches people that they have to find their own moral responsibility toward God through acts of honesty and the search for the absolute truth (*Wahrheitssuche*), even if it means hurting the feelings of others. This emphasis on self reflection and righteousness are, at times, placed higher than harmony with others. Moralistic, confrontational behavior is almost guaranteed.

A conservative tradition

Being right in the middle of Europe, Austria has absorbed contradictory currents of Western democratic thinking and Eastern despotism. The relatively democratic and egalitarian spirit of Western European culture came from free City States like Venice, Frankfurt, Lübeck and Hamburg. People in these cities could question the status quo freely and without fear. They played a decisive role in the development of self-governing independent regions, which eventually evolved into a separation of church and state.

This never happened in Austria. Not one of its cities demonstrated any signs of independence. Vienna, Graz and Innsbruck were originally the residences of local nobles. Then they became administrative centers for the Habsburg rulers. Salzburg belonged to the richest and most powerful archbishop in the German-speaking territories.

Furthermore, historians point out the Habsburgs' approach to governing was that of an alternate mixture of "humanistic absolutism", exemplified by Joseph II, and police-state controls, symbolized by Metternich—a sort of conservative yin-yang arc. The upshot of this is Austrians are more likely to accept the status quo. They historically have never "burned down the house", like the French did in 1789. Rather, through the centuries they have learned to express dissatisfaction indirectly and frustration in a roundabout manner.

To keep their large, multi-cultural empire together for 640 years, Austrians learned to reconcile different ethnic, national and cultural values.

Keeping a multi-cultural empire together

There is a famous Latin proverb that every Austrian schoolchild learns by heart: *Bella gerant ali, tu felix Austria nube!* In German: *Mögen die anderen Länder Kriege führen, Du, glückliches Österreich heirate!* In English: "Let other countries carry out wars—you, lucky Austria, marry!"

This saying probably best describes the Austrian character in a nutshell. They compromise and avoid conflict through charm and beating around the bush. The origins for this behavior can be traced to what it took to maintain the Austro-Hungarian Empire. For 640 years the German-speaking Habsburgs ruled a large territory—consisting of many different ethnic and cultural groups—Hungarians, Romanians, Poles, Czechs, Slovakians, Croatians, Slovenians and Italians.

The ruling elite found out over time that it couldn't just issue orders and decrees and expect to maintain peace. There were too many cultural frictions and tribal issues. To keep this vast empire together at minimal cost and energy, the Habsburgs turned to multi-ethnic reconciliation: listening and compromise. They essentially became "cross-cultural swingers", working with a dozen competing value systems!

Anybody wishing to integrate and work successfully in the Austrian-Hungarian empire, especially in Vienna, had to demonstrate diplomatic skill. Making compliments and softening the truth became the *modus vivendi* of Austrians. Through time, and without realizing it "the country drew a good deal of its strength from the idea of the center, of compromise, exhibiting an almost narcissistic love of the middle way and a leveling of extremes".

This last statement is the key as to why Austrians are unique (and excellent) communicators and explains why they are such successful and subtle negotiators in Eastern Europe and the Far East. They practice a byzantine-like strategy of tipping around firm positions. It's even become official government policy. The Austrian Post Office put out a stamp that proudly states: "Austria is a labyrinth, in which each one finds their way."

Mon Alsace

Fading childhood dreams of a unique Franco-German experience

When I was ten, I spent the summer with my French grandparents in Alsace. I was from suburban Los Angeles and didn't speak French. Nobody in Leimbach, a village on the edge of the Vosges Mountains, spoke English. Culture shock is a mild way to describe my first few weeks!

But those weeks stretched into 15 months. I attended the local *École des garçons,* became fluent in French and far less American in my ideas. Unfortunately, this didn't help during recess when all the kids automatically switched to the German dialect, Alsatian, they spoke at home. That was, as Mark Twain would say, "too many for me."

I was having enough trouble learning one language; Alsatian was out of the question. Nonetheless, strains of it—words and phrases, sound and rhythm—made their way into my ears. And the charm of that unique pocket of Franco-German culture stayed with me.

A decade later I returned to the region for a year as a student at *l'Université de Strasbourg.* And after graduating from the California State University, I went back to Europe, learned German and began working in Stuttgart. I didn't know it but I was well on my way to becoming an interculturalist.

Alsace has very strong connections to German culture as can be seen in the typical architecture.

Which came first, chicken or egg? Was it 15 months in Alsace as a child that gave me the wanderlust to spend my adult life in Germany, Austria, French Canada and Malaysia? Or was there already something inside me, which made those 15 months take such hold? Is it "in ourselves or in our stars?"

Shakespeare says it's the former but I think it's a combination of the two. What is certain is that the cultures we come to be part of, no matter how marginally, become part of us. And so, when my wife and I sat down to discuss the next part of our lives, I remembered Alsace.

Settling down in Strasbourg gave us the best of both worlds. For my wife, who was born and raised in nearby Besançon, it was to return to *la douce France.* But the bridge across the Rhine to Kehl means as much to her as to me. Our years in Germany and Austria—the language and culture we gained there—have left their mark of an adopted homeland.

Settling down in Strasbourg I was also, as a friend of mine likes to say, looking forward to the past. Wondering how much would remain of that year at the university when I was 20. Not just in the changing architecture of stores and cafés, but in the feel of the place—the "vibe", as people from California say.

I remembered that the kids from *l'École des garçons,* thanks to their Alsatian dialect, had gone on to learn German. And that the university itself had a bicultural history: classes were in German when Goethe got his law degree in 1771.

To sum up two millennia briefly, Alsace was home to Germanic tribes from before the Roman invasion and was later part of the Austrian Empire. When France took possession with the Peace of Westphalia in 1648, Louis XIV repeatedly stated *Don't touch the affairs of Alsace.* Commerce and government continued to be conducted in German and, in fact, customs stations excluded Alsatians from official French territory. It was only in 1860, with compulsory schooling, that French language and culture began to influence the populace.

But then it was back to German a decade later, after the Franco-Prussian War. Ironically enough, although most Alsatians didn't speak French, they resented being forced to change their nationality. By 1914, however, Alsace had regained a thoroughly Germanic identity based on both language and geography.

When Paris regained control of the region in 1918, the government attempted to institute unilingual French schools. Alsatians were horrified at losing their cultural identity and a political movement emerged (*Heimatbund*) that was heading toward popular revolt when the French government accepted a de facto bilingual system.

Twenty-two years later, when the Nazis annexed Alsace, a famous poster depicted the future of anyone who refused to reject Gallic culture. Likewise, in 1945, French authorities used the same idea to initiate a campaign to eradicate all traces of Germanic culture in the province. Any child who spoke Alsatian in the schoolyard, much less in the classroom, was severely punished and the parents were suspected of a lack of national loyalty.

This policy is the key to understanding the Alsace of today: denigrating German and the dialect did incalculable damage to the self-esteem of young Alsatians. Research in socialization tells us that children learn culture by internalizing their parents' and teachers' behavior and re-enacting these subjective experiences through role-playing. This is how culture is transmitted. When small children are told in no uncertain terms that their mother tongue is bad, it doesn't take long before the culture disappears. And that is exactly what has happened.

German poster, 1940 (left): The Nazi autorities initiated a policy of eliminating anything French in Alsace. French poster, 1945 (right): The French government copied the idea of sweeping. This meant not only Nazism, but anything German.

Still, that's the thing about redrawn borders: it takes a toll on the people living there. After the Nazis, there were very few Alsatians who wanted anything to do with Germany. In any case, they were French again but continued to speak a form of German at home. And the essential things—cooking, music, jokes—were Germanic, not Latin. But the future was quite obviously French.

In 1970 Strasbourg was a unique pocket of Franco-German culture, but when I returned 40 years later all that had changed. Young Alsatians no longer learn German, they study English instead. Just as with any linguistic culture in the process of disappearing, few understand their grandparents' dialect and even fewer speak it. Two generations of official institutions and media and a culture can all but disappear.

And culture is a big word, a jumble of actions and attitudes. Behavior. These days I drive across to Kehl just for the peace of organized traffic, clean sidewalks and quiet cafés. Then I plunge back across the bridge and, even though I live there, I feel my blood pressure rise in the emotional clamor of Parisian-style driving.

At the end of it all, languages are disappearing in the Global World at an increasing rate. And when the words cease to be spoken, an entire and distinct culture disappears. At the same time, once political movements have more or less homogenized society, they can go back and repair some of the damage. Walking through the campus I once attended, depressed at the extent to which the Alsatians have lost their roots, I thought of the Acadian people I learned about while living in Canada.

In the 1760s, the British deported French-speaking Acadians who refused to pledge allegiance to the King of England. Atlantic Canada was to be an English-speaking region.

The British defeated the French in far-flung Atlantic Canada in 1763. Acadians who refused to pledge allegiance to the king of England were deported to Louisiana (where Acadien became Cajun). For those who remained, life was in English from then on.

Two centuries later a quarter of a million people had managed to keep something of their language and culture alive. It went without saying that most spoke better English, or at least they wrote it better, because there were no French schools. There was no service in French anywhere—not in hospitals or at the Post Office, not in stores or restaurants.

But then, just as the last generation of francophone Acadians was in sight, the federal government finally gave in to local demands. There would be French-language schools, bilingual service in government offices, even in stores and restaurants. The politicians voted in the laws, then spent money on programs designed to make the idea behind those laws come true.

It took less than a generation! Acadian music, theatre and literature exploded. A French-language university opened its doors to a few hundred students and a quarter-century later there were five thousand. Francophone businesses sprang up, just in time to replace the dying traditional trades of farming, fishing and forestry.

This is what I hope for here in Alsace. That both Strasbourg and Paris recognize there's still time to save a language and culture, which was once vibrant and could be again. All it takes is a plan; all it takes is the political will to act. As for the Alsatians, they're both willing and able to meet the challenge, I'm sure. After 40 years as an interculturalist, I'm willing to stake my reputation on it…

"The limits of my language are the limits of my world"

Austrian-British philosopher Ludwig Wittgenstein provides the line I use to introduce the interlocking nature of language and thought and it always leads to a lively discussion. A well-turned phrase transmits the tenets of thought far more effectively than any lecture.

The question of how language shapes the way we think goes back at least a dozen centuries—Charlemagne's "To have a second language is to have a second soul."

Far more recently, Russian linguist Roman Jakobson pointed out "languages differ essentially in what they must convey, not in what they may convey." The power of a mother tongue is not that it allows thought but that it forces it! Think about the following sentence:

I talked to my neighbor last night.

If I were speaking French of German, I'd have to choose *voisin* or *voisine, Nachbar* or *Nachbarin*. Gender-based tongues make for more specific images, while anglophones aren't required to consider the sexes of people they refer to.

Language is not only a communication tool; it's a system, which allows us to organize perception and subsequent thinking. The American linguist Benjamin Whorf posited that we act in certain ways because our mental patterns are shaped by how we speak. In other words, our language habits play a powerful role in conditioning our way of thinking and viewing reality.

How we express ourselves on a day-to-day basis reflects what we decide is critical to survival and adaptation. Americans act quickly because their mindset tells them "time is money" while *la dolce vita* leaves Italians smiling… when they're not waving their arms in argument.

Even saying *No* is relative, as demonstrated by a Hong Kong journalist's delightful piece of satire:

CHINESE EDITOR'S REJECTION LETTER
We have read your manuscript with boundless delight. If we were to publish your paper, however, it would then be impossible for us

to publish any work of a lower standard. And it is unthinkable that in the next thousand years we shall see its equal. We are, to our regret, compelled to return your divine composition and to beg you one thousand times to overlook our short-sighted timidity.

Regardless of ethnicity, my students are always amused when they read this but there is a difference. Europeans and Americans could never imagine writing anything even approaching that sort of approach… Whereas the Chinese, Japanese and Indian members of my workshops flatly state that they could (and would).

Westerners and Asians may share a common experience when confronted with the mechanisms of rejection and face-saving but each experiences "a kaleidoscopic flux of impressions that has to be organized by our mind—and this means mostly by the linguistic system of our mind" (Benjamin Whorf).

Because saving face is so deeply embedded in their mental pathways, the Chinese possess a formidable array of honorific expressions. And it's a rhetoric for which the West has no patience.

People from different cultures don't think alike—that we know. What we understand less is the degree to which the language in which we learn to survive acts as a continual translator of reality.

Words define the constructs, which cause friction when we attempt to understand foreign values or new ways. Language defines our nature.

The story of the *Tower of Babel* recounts the efforts of united humanity metaphorically attempting to achieve a godlike status. God is not amused and His answer strikes a universal chord. One tongue becomes a thousand—the mind-numbing cacophony of man-as-monkey—and the tower is no more.

The story is obviously a mirror (as befit the parables of those biblical times) representing the war-or-peace choice tribes have when dealing with one another.

Every person on the planet may well be connected on an existential level; it all goes back to families, clans, tribes and nations. We're each condemned to perceive our own realities and to express what we feel in a very specific way… which is often only vaguely understood by "outsiders".

Taking a dynamic *other* perspective necessitates a leap of consciousness. Back-and-forth communication is problematic at best amidst a "clash of differing realities."

And so we're led back to the most fundamental questions of intercultural studies. How do we become the way we are? What makes us think the way we do? How can we relate to people from outside our tribe in a more relevant way?

The answers are found in the language we speak.

"The awful German language"

Mark Twain's most famous ethnocentric essay revisited and updated

Mark Twain gave his country a voice by writing in the idioms and rhythms of the people. Huckleberry Finn and Tom Sawyer—two characters he created out of the clay of Hannibal, Missouri—are beloved all over the world. But the "father of American literature" was not a full-time novelist; he spent as much time writing short stories and satirical essays, one of the funniest being *The Awful German Language.*

Twain was trying to master the "devilish tongue" in Heidelberg back in 1879 and his frustration found an outlet in mocking the overly-complicated grammar. On a more profound level he was in culture shock, dealing with a radically different pattern of thought, and his proto-linguistic critique was the happy result.

In fact, he enjoyed learning German and eventually became somewhat fluent. Years later, while living in Vienna, he was granted a private audience

Mark Twain at work, writing out his frustrations.

with Kaiser Franz-Joseph. Twain planned to impress the emperor and prepared a speech in German. Unfortunately, when the big day came, he froze in the imperial presence and was unable to remember his lines!

Three-quarters of a century later, my own attempt at German was similar enough to Mr. Twain's that I decided to update and rewrite his brilliant study of German logic.

Many people wanting to learn German as a foreign language have absolutely no idea what the proverb *Deutsche Sprache, schwere Sprache* really means. For the foreign student trying to master this language, it often seems like a mysterious logic of communication designed to go against every rule of good common sense.

For example, to be taken seriously in the German language, one needs to conceal the meaning of a sentence by placing the main verb at the very end. Read the following excerpt (literally translated) from a recent newspaper article:

The government announced today, that the Finance Minister the new income tax system because of its new format with a self fill-in procedure, which many outside observers it fairer describe, and its simpler write off system, already in other European countries applied, from the first of January of the new year introduced be will.

Although it is supposed to be eloquent, it sounds more like Teutonic verse gone amok, leaving the foreign reader both confused and stunned.

This may explain why Germans have a tic, "temporary paralysis", frequently noticed by foreigners. It seems when Germans are listening to someone, they are intensely waiting for the speaker to tell them the last word. And when it is finally announced, you see an expression of climactic relief on their faces. However, should the iPhone ring or the baby start crying before the verb arrives, they often miss the meaning of the sentence. Then the poor German is left hanging with a large, incomplete sentence in his head, frustrated in not knowing what was said.

This obsession with the verb at the end leads to comical situations. Imagine the following. A young man, let us call him Hans, is declaring his love to a young woman. The phrase *Ich habe mich in dich verliebt* goes something like this: "Gretchen, my feelings are so strong that I for the reasons of the beauty of your eyes, your little rosebud mouth, your thoroughly-trained, sporty body and last but not least your sexy Marlene Dietrich voice, with you in love fallen have." Unfortunately, Gretchen had to answer the ringing doorbell midway through this rambling discourse, and never heard the magic verb. Tragedy strikes again.

But if that isn't bad enough, the German language compounds the problem with the large number of verbs. The general rule, as far as I can make out, is the more the merrier. Therefore, German sentences have lots of *haben sind gewesen gehabt worden können geworden sein.* It really sounds like a musical merry-go-around, allowing Germans to make themselves sound self-important, but it is not supposed to be taken at all seriously.

Even more awkward is the German habit of putting many words into one. The words *Donaudampfschiffahrtgesellschaftskapitän* or *Entbindungsstationsschwesternaufenthaltsraum* are gigantic, mumbo-jumbo sayings, whose sole function is to terrify the unfortunate foreign language student into thinking that the learning of German is a hopeless cause from the very beginning!

The German language's handling of the gender, or how nouns are classified according to sex, is total chaos. Take, for example, the noun *Sonne* (sun), which symbolizes power, destruction, force. For some inexplicable reason, it has the feminine gender *die.*

The noun *Mond* (moon), on the other hand, which is the symbol of tranquility, intuition and passivity is given the masculine gender *der*.

But the biggest surprise is the classification of the nouns "young girl" and "heart", which are given the neutral gender *das*, presumably to indicate that they are not supposed to have any sex at all! How the poor foreign student is able to detect logic in this ridiculous classification system is beyond me.

However, the ultimate tragedy of a language system gone mad are the word endings. When someone wishes to express something in German, each part of the sentence must first be thoroughly analysed, so that the word endings have proper inflections. To understand the system requires a monumental intellectual effort that only a masochistic genius might want to attempt. Take the simple phrase "the big hamburger", which in German is *der grosse Hamburger*. If this is in the accusative case, then it becomes *den grossen Hamburger*. Using the preposition "with", it changes to the dative and the endings change— *mit dem grossen Hamburger*. "The catsup of the big hamburger" is the genitive case or the possessive, which in German is *der Ketchup des grossen Hamburgers*.

At this point, the person attempting to speak German begins to feel a sense of numb horror. But dealing with the plural is even worse, further traumatizing the already linguistically battered student. Rather than to continue tormenting your mind, it is better to enter a MacDonald's restaurant in Germany and give your order for a big hamburger in plain simple English than to stumble around in this grammatical hodge-podge.

The discreet horrors
of learning the English language

Let me state a simple fact: the teaching of English has become the world's fastest growing industry. Classrooms are jammed with millions of eager learners wishing to master and speak this language, which was considered as "the inadequate and second rate tongue of peasants" for centuries. Then the Beatles came along. Today English has become the most important language in the world.

But few people realize how difficult it is for all but native speakers to follow its complexities. Combat-hardened teachers will tell you that, despite the universal impression that learning English is easy, it is not. For most students, the language appears to be an incoherent code of inconsistencies, a total disaster from a learning point of view.

Hard to believe? Think about the simple phrase used when meeting people for the first time—"How do you do?"

How do I do what? It's impeccable logic but the questioner will be taken aback if you reply that way. Upon analysis, not only is the question horribly incomplete, but the standard answer—to simply say "How do you do" back—makes no sense at all.

This is only for starters. Trying to teach phonetic and spelling rules to a foreigner can best be described as grotesque. For instance, if an English teacher went to the blackboard and wrote an agglomeration of letters like *tchst,* *sthm,* and *tchph,* you would think two things: 1. these letters are totally unpronounceable. 2. the teacher must be crazy. Yet these letters are used every day in words like *matchstick,* *asthma,* and *catchphrase.*

Despite so-called phonetic rules, the odds of pronouncing words correctly are almost as bad as those of hitting the jackpot in Las Vegas.

The following examples demonstrate the absurdities:

Written		Pronounced
ache	=	ayk
busy	=	bizi
bury	=	beri
enough	=	in af
read	=	red or ri:d

Then you have the problem of which pronunciation is correct. Consider a "girl" on an around-the-world tour. In the U.S. and Canada, she'd be *gurl,* but a *gel* in England and Australia, a *gull* in Ireland, a *gill* in South Africa and a *gairull* in Scotland.

The obvious conclusion is that the English spelling-versus-pronunciation relationship is so treacherously erratic, it's a waste of time to think of rules. The best strategy is simply to stumble on hoping someday to understand the language's shameless, yet charming, contradictions.

Another wrinkle which adds insult to injury is the learner's being caught in the middle of the American-British firing line concerning correct usage. And it's not like the two are similar. Most people listening to the BBC News would describe the tone as refined, sophisticated, spoken by the elite. News reporters on American networks are far more caffeine-fed and often sound like nervous sportscasters.

Historically, the British have always felt superior in their use of the language. Infamous satirist Samuel Johnson voiced popular contempt in 1769, describing Americans as "a race of convicts and ought to be thankful for anything we allow them short of hanging".

Agree or not, you're forced to learn that, in Britain, one writes *programme, favour, cheque* and *night,* whereas in America it's *program, favor, check* and, on commercial signs, *nite.* Should you have the bad luck to use British spelling in America, or vice-versa, you might well be scolded or in the worst scenario tarred and feathered, an experience I would wish on no one.

And then there's *legalese,* which can be added to the list of the world's greatest tortures. Lawyers are proud of their precise formulations but basically it's mumbo-jumbo, double-talk—terms like "the party of the first part", "for and on behalf of" and "including but not exclusive to". It is as if lawyers do not understand each other without these meaningless redundancies, but worse of all, students have to learn this if they have to sign contracts in English.

Then again, the problems mentioned above are peanuts compared with the famous "present perfect"—a nightmare for English teachers and a veritable Waterloo for their students, all of whom think a sentence like "We are in London since four days" is absolutely splendid and pleasing to the ear. They don't understand the look of shock on the faces of English-speakers upon hearing it.

When I explain the right way to say it is "We have been in London for four days", students seem to think I'm suffering from some strange disease. Not only do they find the rule hard to accept, they insist they've never heard of it… no matter how many times it's repeated. Still, if a teacher has great patience and a winning personality, a miracle sometimes occurs and students eventually use the present perfect correctly.

Finally, the mistake that drives English teachers everywhere right up the wall is the fetish of putting "would" in the subordinate clause of a conditional sentence. *If I would be rich, I would be happier* is guaranteed to make English-speakers wince in pain but, once again, students are blithely unaware of the fingernails-on-blackboard sound. *If they were to use their ears, they would have an easier time of it.*

Which brings me back to my main point: due to its incoherent, crazy logic, English is an extremely difficult language. Learning it should be limited to those who possess exceptional intelligence coupled with a high resistance to frustration. But how does one identify such exceptional people?

Are you still reading?—You're one of them.

Some interesting facts
about bilingualism

To have another language is to possess a second soul.
Charlemagne 742 – 814

One characteristic that makes the intercultural field different from other professions is the relatively high percentage of facilitators who have spoken two or more languages fluently since early childhood. Research indicates those who grow up bilingual are able to:

· learn new words easily
· use information in new ways
· resolve conflicts and ambiguities more harmoniously
· better connect with others (listening skills)

Bilingualism seems to have a profound effect on the brain, lasting well into the twilight years, and even improves certain cognitive skills not related to language. How is it that the words and phrases we hear and speak have such a heavy impact? This is what the research tells us:

System interference: Neuroscientific experiments on bilingual persons demonstrate clearly that both languages are working simultaneously, even when only one language is being used. This means one language is blocking the other but this is actually a blessing in disguise — because neurons are required to obstruct signals from the second language, the cognitive muscles of the brain are given a "positive" workout.

These reinforced cognitive muscles, in turn, refine the brain's management function, an ordering system for directing attention, solving problems and performing other complex tasks. Examples include ignoring distractions, remaining focused and remembering information, which explains how actors are able to play Hamlet and Lear.

It would seem that the advantage bilinguals have over monolinguals stems primarily from a heightened ability to monitor one's environment. As a Spanish researcher pointed out, "Bilinguals have to switch languages quite often — you may talk to your mother in Spanish and your father in German." The continual demand to keep track of changes is similar to the way people observe the traffic when driving.

A fascinating study in the South-Tyrol compared the ability to monitor tasks on the part of German-Italian bilinguals and Italian monolinguals. The bilingual subjects not only performed better, they were also more efficient, doing so with less effort.

Linguistic Relativity and Personality Changes: The language people speak shapes the way they see the world. Since bilingual people possess two linguistic realities, they have a broader, more diverse way of perceiving phenomena. One's personality is also broader. Ziao-lei Wang writes in her book *Growing up with Three Languages: Birth to Eleven:*

One reason for Canada's positive image in the world is its bilingualism.

"Languages used by speakers with one or more than one language are used not just to represent a unitary self, but to enact different kinds of selves, and different linguistic contexts create different kinds of self-expression and experiences for the same person."

Generating the appropriate personality may be the reason bilingual people get high scores on tests for personality traits such as cultural empathy, open-mindedness and social initiative. A country like Canada, for example, with 30 % of its people speaking both French and English, is more open to others, which has contributed to its positive image in the world. This form of contextual self-expression is best summarized by linguist Francois Grosjean: "What's seen as a change in personality is most probably simply a shift in attitudes and behaviors that correspond to a shift in situation or context, independent of language."

Critical period: Mastering the high-level semantic aspects of a language implies an understanding of the culture and history in which that language evolved. Children using a second language in the "critical period" up to age 11 or 12 normally assimilate its cultural assumptions, something which doesn't usually occur after that period. A person may know a language fluently but, if the cultural knowledge is lacking, it's a very good way to make a "fluent fool" of oneself. This is where intercultural trainers come into play—making participants aware of the values and assumptions of the target-culture as well as their own.

Firewall against dementia: Bilingualism seems to affect the brain well into our senior years. Researchers at the University of California, San Diego, studied 44 elderly Spanish-English bilinguals and found those who were fluent in both were less susceptible to dementia and Alzheimer's disease. Their conclusion was that the better one is at speaking two languages, the later the onset of cognitive disintegration.

While the advantages of bilingualism are obvious in terms of the development of the brain, as well as social skills, this is not an end in itself. Nothing is more exciting than the actual experience of talking to new people in their mother tongue, understanding the background buzz of conversations on foreign streets, reading a great book in the language it was written in, or watching a classic film without subtitles.

This is why basically everyone on the planet is exhilarated by the intercultural experience of speaking another language, and why most describe it—in whatever language—as "mind-blowing".

"Let the inmates run the asylum"

Thiagi's philosophy and methods on learning

I had the opportunity recently to take part in a three-day workshop put on by the brilliant game creator, Sivasailam "Thiagi" Thiagarajan. He practices what he preaches, namely that real learning occurs when the students do most of the work. Or, as Thiagi humorously put it, "let the inmates run the asylum."

And he means it literally. The very first minute you step into the classroom, Thiagi announces you're going to play a game called "Hello". The participants are split into teams, which are assigned one of four questions based on past experience, expectations, future projects and personal interest. Each group had three minutes to plan how to collect the responses, three minutes for doing so, and three minutes for analyzing the data and one minute to present the findings.

Once this icebreaker started, we were running around like chickens with our heads cut off, not knowing where the exercise would take us. But, as Thiagi pointed out, it replaced "the boredom of sitting down and listening to an introductory lecture." It also set the tone for the next three days. Students took part in one game after another, making for incredible fun, while slowly reinforcing the idea that the best learning is done as a social process.

In Thiagi's world, effective training means designing activities so that participants do the work; they gain knowledge and skills rather than merely receiving information. Or, as seen from a Chinese perspective, acquiring knowledge is the interplay of content and activity—a sort of yin-yang movement.

Some of the principles are:
· adult students bring a wealth of experience to sessions
· peer-teaching is a powerful technique
· students don't consume teaching, they create it
· actively responding produces more effective learning than
  passively listening or reading.

Another important aspect is proper debriefing. Thiagi says that while experience may be the best teacher, raw experience doesn't guarantee learning. An experience is long lasting only when we have reflected on it, gained insights and shared them with others. A facilitator should follow up with the following questions:

1. How do you feel?
2. What happened?
3. What did you learn?
4. How does it relate to your work?
5. What if? (the activity had been in another situation)
6. What next? (improved strategies for future activities)

Thiagi's methods may be based on simple cognitive rules and ageless common sense, but his effortlessly entertaining style makes him the supreme Master—the "Mozart of Games".

Discovering the
"Intercultural Development Inventory" (IDI) *

A reliable and valid measure of intercultural competence

I'd like to begin this talk by telling you a story. It's about Jürgen, a young, brilliant executive, working for one of Germany's automobile companies. Now, I say brilliant because by the age of 27, Jürgen had already become the personal assistant to the CEO. He was not only quick and super-smart, but was also perceived as being flexible, open-minded and always accomplished his tasks with 110% Teutonic efficiency. The Board of Directors liked Jürgen and felt he had a high potential to become a Member of the Board. But they told him he needed to round off his skills with a two- or three-year foreign assignment. So, they decided to name him CFO at their Brazilian subsidiary. This was an extraordinary promotion for such a young person. As preparation, Jürgen and his wife were given four weeks of Portuguese language training. Then, it was off to São Paulo, where he took on his new responsibilities with great enthusiasm.

First day on the job Jürgen found, to his complete surprise, that the people in the finance department didn't keep all records of price changes. At that time, Brazil was suffering from run-away inflation of about 1100% per year, which meant prices were changed four to five times a day. When he asked his Brazilian subordinates why they didn't keep all financial records, they just replied, "We don't have time to note all the price changes. But don't worry; we know what we are doing. We always make money." Jürgen didn't like this disorderly way of doing things. Guided by his German value *Ordnung muß sein,* he ordered them to write down all price changes. To no avail. His Brazilian staff refused to change their methods. This battle of who was going to set policy went on for six weeks. Finally, after seeing he couldn't get them to change, Jürgen threw in the towel and flew back to Germany.

Because of this fiasco abroad, Jürgen's future career prospects had been put on hold. But worst, he became the laughing stock of the whole company. People were saying, "Ha, ha, ha. He thought he was so smart and yet, when he was sent abroad, he failed miserably."

What conclusions can we draw from this story? I think there are two: Although Jürgen was confident, highly intelligent, and possessed a strong will to see projects through, he was short of the most important skill when dealing with foreigners—intercultural

---

* This is a shortened version of a talk given at the SIETAR Europa Congress in Granada, Spain, Oct., 2008

sensitivity, that is the ability to communicate and behave appropriately in a new culture. No one had made him aware before his departure that he would unconsciously project and try to impose his German cultural values on to the Brazilians.

The second conclusion is that if your orientation to cultural differences is not made clear before going abroad, huge and expensive fiascos are guaranteed.

This is where the *Intercultural Development Inventory* comes in. More commonly known as the IDI, it's a short paper and pencil survey of an individual's sensitivity to cultural differences. If, before his departure, Jürgen had been given feedback on his intercultural preferences by means of the IDI, it would have promoted greater self-awareness and lowered potential misunderstandings.

Now, what does IDI do exactly? It measures your orientation to cultural difference and the results are transformed into an in-depth graphic profile, which indicates where you are in terms of intercultural development. And when I talk about intercultural development, I mean, whether your worldview is ethnocentric—perceiving your reality only from your own cultural perspective or ethnorelative, which means you're comfortable with many standards and customs in different cultures.

The IDI was developed by both Milton Bennett and Mitch Hammer over a six-year-period. Since then it has been piloted and implemented in corporate and educational settings, proving to be a reliable and valid measure of intercultural competence.

Immediately people raise the question: how can you measure intercultural competence in a reliable, that is consistent, and valid way? Do the test results mirror actual intercultural competence? If we define intercultural competence as the ability to communicate and behave appropriately in a new culture, can you empirically measure this ability? The answer is yes if we are to use Milton Bennett's *Developmental Model of Intercultural Sensitivity,* more commonly known as the DMIS.

Published in 1986, the DMIS is a theoretical framework that explains how people make sense of cultural differences and their reaction to them. Dr. Bennett observed in both the academic and corporate worlds that individuals confronted cultural difference in predictable ways. Based on this observation he made the following assumption: as your experience of cultural difference becomes more complex and sophisticated, your competence in intercultural relations increases.

The framework is organized along a developmental continuum of six stages. If you look at the image on page 22, you can see the first three are ethnocentric and the last three are categorized as ethnorelative.

Each stage indicates a particular perceptional mode and behavior. By recognizing the underlying cognitive orientation toward culture difference, you can make predictions about people's behavior and training can be tailored to facilitate development into the next stage. This model is considered by many intercultural professionals as the best explanation of what an individual goes through when developing intercultural competence.

The six stages in more detail

Denial is the most basic form of ethnocentrism. Your outlook is essentially parochial. You assume that your cultural reality is the only real one and there are no real differences among people from other cultures. You're comfortable with your familiar surroundings and not eager to complicate your existence with cultural differences.

Although you might be a witness to a tremendous number of foreign cultural experiences, you generally fail to make something out of them. That is, there is no successive construing and re-construing of unfamiliar events: they are simply not being registered. An example of this sort of aggressive ignorance might be seen among some American high school students, who, for the first time, go abroad to Germany. They have just come back home after a one-week stay in Munich and are asked about their impressions of Germany. They say it's "just like home". When questioned what they meant by that, the reply might be, "Well, Munich has lots of buildings, too many cars and McDonald's."

Or another example is the experience of an American technician who I had as a participant in one of my intercultural trainings. His name was Gary and he came from a small mid-West town called Plymouth, located in the state of Indiana. A German company set up operations in his area and he was hired and sent to Germany to do company training for six weeks. This was his first time out of the United States. Two weeks after his return, I asked him about differences he might have noticed between Americans and Germans. Gary replied that there weren't any. Surprised, I said, "You must have observed some differences." Again, he stated emphatically there weren't any. A German in the class was astonished by what he heard and insisted that he must have observed some differences. Finally, Gary said: "Well, the Germans seem to be bit more precise than Americans." After hearing that, I thought about his statement and drew the following conclusion: when Gary was in Germany, he probably felt so overwhelmed and threatened by cultural differences that he reacted by denying his German experiences, in order to protect his identity.

Defensive is the next stage. Here, you don't deny cultural differences—on the contrary, you're conscious of them, but you generally don't like them. These differences are considered a threat to your self-esteem and identity. As a result of this, you often create negative stereotypes in order to promote an internal feeling of superiority and the "rightness"

People in the defensive stage see their culture as superior to all others, as depicted in this amusing 18th century etching of British-French rivalary.

of your own value system. In other words, your own culture is experienced as the only good one and all others are inferior.

Let me give you an example of this. I often do intercultural training for German engineers who have just started to live and work in the USA. The scenario is often the same: at first they're euphoric about being in the USA, but after a few months, culture shock kicks in and suddenly these engineers find themselves lost and disoriented. So, what do they do to counteract these feelings? They become highly critical of the USA, irrationally placing their frustration and anxiety onto the host nation. Defensive statements are often made, such as: "Americans are superficial and uncultivated" or "We could teach these Americans a lot about being orderly."

There's a variation to this called reversal. A person in the reversal stage has a largely positive view of their newly adopted culture and a somewhat negative opinion of their own native culture. An example is that of a young Peace Corp volunteer, who is sent to Costa Rica. After six months there, he or she thinks it is better than the USA. People say that person has "gone native". According to Milton Bennett, the reversal orientation is the "mirror image" of the defense orientation and therefore also ethnocentric.

The DMIS predicts that as time goes by, people move from the defensive into the *Minimization* stage. As the term suggests, cultural differences are minimized or trivialized, while at the same time there's an emphasis on how people are all similar and a belief in the universality of basic values.

But you're still essentially obscuring deep cultural differences because your notions of universality are defined in terms of your own culture. To illustrate this, let's assume you're a Peace Corp volunteer in a Peruvian village. You firmly believe there's a universal need to be successful and the people in this village should be grateful that you are teaching them this. When you find that Peruvians don't identify with this value, you might react by saying, "Why can't they be just like us Americans?"

Other typical statements of universality are, "We are all children of God" or "I have this intuitive sense of other people, no matter what their culture is." There's also this belief of just being yourself and human will suffice.

When you are in the minimization state, you're excessively respectful of other cultures and see yourself as well-meaning and kind. You seek to avoid stereotypes by viewing and judging others as individuals. Today, we call this being "politically correct".

However, in many cases, you aren't aware that you might be a member of a dominant culture with institutional privileges. At the SIETAR Congress in Sofia in 2006, Hungarian and Bulgarians members told about their contacts with Western European and American business people. They wanted to introduce (in reality impose) Western business methods in Eastern Europe. These Westerners were polite, respectful and saw themselves as being open with good intentions. They would downplay differences by making remarks, like "We business people are the same all over the world." What they didn't realize was that they were members of a dominant culture that had the economic upper-hand and could dictate what was going to be done. Consequently, they were perceived by the local population as privileged, patronizing and imperialistic.

Acceptance is the first of the three ethnorelative stages. Here, there is a fundamental shift in the mindset from the unconscious assumption that your culture is the definer of reality to a more conscious assumption that your own culture is just one of many, equally complex worldviews.

Acceptance does not mean agreement—some behavior may be judged as immoral and repugnant—but your judgment is no more ethnocentric. Rather, there's an acceptance of cultural differences in verbal and non-verbal behavior. You come to the realization that the ideas, feelings and behavior of others are just as rich as yours. In this stage, you are curious about other cultures and enjoy recognizing and exploring differences.

I noted this behavior while conducting intercultural trainings for American college students who came to Germany on a four-month exchange program. By the end of the program, most students had a better understanding of Germans, but were not quite out of the minimization stage because their stay in Germany was too short for any significant transformation to occur. However, in one of my classes, one student fell in love with a German during her stay. Suddenly, her attitude was changed from an American ethnocentric outlook to a strong urge to learn everything about Germans and Germany. She told me enthusiastically: "I want to learn the German language and culture well so I can understand my Hans better."

Adaptation is the second ethnorelative stage. It involves a more proactive, conscious effort to internalize other cultural realities. At this stage, you have the ability to "step into another person's shoes". It's a form of empathy, role reversal, where you intentionally shift your frame of reference for the purpose of connecting. Your goal is to maximize communication with people from other cultures.

I lived five years in Montreal, a fascinating bicultural and bilingual city of Francophones and Anglophones. The two groups usually don't get along that well and normally live in separate communities. Despite that, there are some inter-marriages and the children of these culturally-mixed unions develop a worldview with two cultural frameworks. They could be mingling with their Anglophone friends, speaking English and behaving in their Anglo mode and should a Francophone appear, they could immediately shift into the French mode and switch to the French language: "As I was saying... Oh, salut Jean, comment vas tu?"

Integration is the final ethnorelative stage. It could be described as a continual shifting of different cultural worldviews. You're what I call, "cross-cultural swingers", juggling two or more competing value-systems. You're capable of seeing and feeling the relativity of beliefs — you feel there is no absolute standard of "rightness" because you use multiple frames of reference. This can cause you to lose your primary cultural identity and create what might be described as internal cultural shock — existing on the periphery of two or more cultures, what Milton Bennett calls a sort of cultural marginality. This is common among long-term expatriates, "global nomads" and "third-culture kids".

The Czech writer Milan Kundera coined the phrase, "the unbearable lightness of being" to describe how life is ultimately insignificant. When you add "intercultural" at the end, it becomes "the unbearable lightness of being intercultural". Long-term expatriates will smile and say "Yeah, that sort of describes my mental state." Despite the periodic confusion in their identity, people in the integration stage will often say, "I truly enjoy participating in all these cultures".

Now that you have become familiar with the DMIS, we can look into the actual administering of the *Intercultural Development Inventory,* which can be given to individuals or groups. Before the IDI is passed out, the respondents are given a short introductory talk on the meaning of intercultural sensitivity and the challenges facing cultural differences. The actual DMIS is not explained at this stage.

The IDI is then handed out. As said earlier, it's a paper and pencil instrument composed of 50 statements, each statement reflecting a different stage of the DMIS. For example "People are fundamentally the same despite apparent differences in cultures" or "I feel rootless because I do not think I have a cultural identification." It takes about 20 to 30 minutes to complete. Responses are scored on a one-to-five-point Likert-type scale. For instance, take the statement: "I like people from different cultures." If you "agree" fully with this, you would fill in the number "5". If you "disagree somewhat more than agree", you would fill in the number "2" and so on.

The results are then compiled into a special computer software, which in turns generates an in-depth graphic and textual profile of an individual or group's predominant stage of intercultural development. When the respondents received their results, they invariably ask, "what does this mean for me?" and a process of self-reflection begins. This phase is what people find the most fascinating because they're discovering and learning about themselves, leading to increased intercultural sensitivity.

Additionally, the IDI also indicates how you rate yourself in terms of intercultural sensitivity. It's important for administrators to have a sense of the discrepancies on how a person rates their perceived strengths in intercultural sensitivity versus the more objective assessment provided by the IDI.

A frequent question asked is how did Dr. Bennett and Dr. Hammer find the statements that would reliably measure intercultural sensitivity. When they started the project back in 1993, the two researchers conducted extensive interviews with 40 international people about their experiences with cultural diversity. Four raters then categorized the interviewees' statements, according to the different stages of DMIS. It was then reviewed by a team of seven experts who removed those items that were not similarly classified by at least five of the seven experts. This resulted in an inventory of 145 statements that corresponded to five of the six DMIS stages. Later, they were then tested on a sample of 226 international respondents, which resulted in the final set of 50 statements. This whole period of developing and refining the IDI spanned six years.

The IDI should be viewed as an instrument that captures how the person tends to think and feel about cultural differences. It measures cognitive structures, that is, how a person construes and organizes events, rather than attitudes. This makes it more stable and less susceptible to situational factors.

Important here, it doesn't compare behaviors. Most other tests of "intercultural competence" are criterion-references, in that they compare in terms of percentages how closely the respondent matches a set of behaviors thought to be associated with intercultural competence. Consistency and quality for such tests are more difficult to establish.

The IDI has met the standard scientific criteria for a valid and reliable psychometric instrument. The editors of *The International Journal of Intercultural Relations* conducted an in-depth analysis of the instrument, and concluded that "it reasonably approximates the developmental model of intercultural sensitivity". The IDI is also related to other standardized tests. The three ethnorelative stages—acceptance, adaptation and integration—correlate positively with the *Worldmindedness Scale*. Likewise, the ethnocentric stages—denial, defence and minimization—correlate positively with the *Intercultural Anxiety Scale*.

This was a short and quick overview of how the IDI measures intercultural sensitivity. Perhaps the most positive outcome of this inventory is that you develop a greater self-awareness about your openness to other cultures. For this reason, the IDI has the added benefit of being both an assessment instrument and a potential vehicle to promote intercultural skill development.

"Germans don't smile at us"
Teaching Americans the German mindset

"In one sentence, give me your first impression of Germany," I asked my American students on the opening day of class. The most popular answer was surprising in its simplicity: "Germans don't smile at us when we smile at them." Thus was the tone set for the three-month course I taught for four years in Köln, in collaboration with AHA International and the University of Oregon.

I like to describe newly arrived American students as good-hearted, with a sunny-boy eagerness to learn everything about their new surroundings. Yet, as with all students abroad, underneath the optimistic veneer is an ethnocentric mindset. In addition to being relatively clueless to German ways, they rarely question their own cultural assumptions.

To borrow an image from a fairy tale, they're like babes in the woods, sticking close together for fear of the big bad wolf and hoping they'll somehow stumble back to civilization. But it's exactly this condition that provides an intercultural facilitator the opportunity to thrive.

So, how does one design a program to transform impressionable young adults into cross-cultural navigators? Or, as the course objectives state, to "bring the students to a higher level of understanding of the host culture, their own culture and themselves."

After a short introduction, I break the ice with an exercise from Robert Kohls' book *Developing Intercultural Awareness*. A form has to be filled out from right to left, nothing more than that, but it shocks the students into awareness of how fundamentally different cultures can be, triggering disorientation and frustration. Further, it demonstrates that even the most mindless of tasks is culturally conditioned.

Going from the strange to what should be—but isn't—familiar, the next bump in the road is *Body Ritual among the Nacirema,* a pseudo-anthropological essay by Horace Miner. The author uses complicated academic jargon to describe a supposedly exotic tribe on the North American continent. In fact, it's a through-the-looking-glass portrait of suburban America (and the name of the tribe is a mirror image as well). Time and time again, I'm amazed that only about a third of the class gets it; the others go on at length about how they're happy not to live in such an "oppressive" culture.

Right about now, the students' self-esteem is hitting a new low so it's the perfect time to introduce the concept of "culture shock". Although they claim to know the term, very few of them actually understand it. I spend a considerable amount of time explaining the different stages of the phenomenon and how a lack of familiar cues leads to a loss of sense of self.

On the other hand, personal evolution takes place through a series of slow but sure "adjustment phases". It's important to spell this out at the beginning because, otherwise, students are often confused about what's happening around them. Unconscious anxiety may lead them to withdraw into an extreme and irrational defensive mode, something I learned with my first group.

They'd been in Köln for about four weeks when I was asked to give them a look at a different city, nearby Düsseldorf. At the end of our visit, I took them to the oldest restaurant in town so they could try the local beer and have a snack. To my surprise, they were hesitant about ordering food. They waited until I asked for potato soup with sausage, then they all asked for the same thing.

It took me a while to figure out what was going on but, as usual, it was childishly simple behavior. Because dogs are allowed in German restaurants, the students (in their depressed stage of culture shock) had collectively developed the phobia that German food wasn't hygienic. I learned that they'd been eating most of their meals at McDonald's, Pizza Hut, Burger King and Subway! Ever since then, I've made a point of explaining culture shock at the very beginning of the course.

Probably the best feedback I get from my students is the DIE (description/interpretation/evaluation) method they use to write a journal, analyzing 25 cross-cultural experiences. The process of distinguishing what they perceive, making sense of it, then giving their opinion on it is a powerful tool for self-discovery. With practice, students can move from self-awareness to awareness of "the other", questioning their own ethnocentric perceptions and gradually becoming aware of cultural and personal relativity.

One stunning admission came from an extremely intelligent young woman who talked about early encounters with her host family. On the first evening, she was uncomfortable when the family spent over an hour at the dinner table, doing more talking than eating. On the second evening she quickly finished her meal and excused herself, returning to her room to "do something useful" and "not waste time." What she ended up doing, however, was watch MTV by herself. When she realized she unconsciously put television on a higher level than being with people, it came as a shock. Or, as she put it, "a mind-blowing revelation".

I used her story as the basis for a discussion on American individualism and the idea that "time is money" as opposed to German collectivism and *Unterhalten* (discussing things in a cosy setting). These traits form a conceptual framework, which helped students comprehend the basic lifestyle they faced in Köln.

"Culture" itself presents an interesting challenge. American emphasis on being unique, on self-realization, leads many students to say, "I'm my own person." They imply that culture doesn't play much of a role in their behavior—a ludicrous notion, albeit a popular one. Americans do share attitudes and beliefs, obviously, but most of my students haven't ever given much thought to their common values. And the next assignment is designed to bring that point home...

"Tonight, at supper, ask your host family if the United States has culture." Of course the answer often comes as a total surprise. Germans (and Europeans, for that matter) may well say, "No, you don't have what we think of as culture. Our nation has far more history than yours, which makes us more mature, more refined. You're like undisciplined teenagers, full of energy, but inexperienced and sometimes dangerously naïve."

As the weeks pass, we look at other concepts of intercultural communication, such as Hofstede and Hall's theoretical frameworks and non-verbal signals, as well as Milton Bennett's *Development Model of Intercultural Sensitivity.* There are also open-book quizzes to make sure concepts are understood. Finally, my students analyze four case studies and have some fun playing exaggerated American and German roles.

By the end of term, a noticeable transformation can be seen. Students are astonished to find that, almost without being aware of it, they've moved from an ethnocentric outlook to a more nuanced and open approach. They're comfortable with the relativity of values and customs. Best of all, they have the vocabulary to articulate this new sensitivity.

Perhaps the best proof of the subtle change in outlook came during a farewell dinner. A popular language teacher

American students at the farewell dinner.

made a speech encouraging them to continue learning German and ended on a somewhat ironic note. "As you now know, we Germans can and do smile."

My students' faces lit up with the glow of intercultural maturity.

Deconstructing the "Empathy Craze"

As any good practitioner of intercultural training will tell you, empathy is deeply embedded in — and inseparable from — intercultural and interpersonal sensitivity. It's a way of conscious-shifting, extending one's boundaries, or as Milton Bennett puts it, an "attempt to understand others by participating in their different experience of the world". The ability to adapt is key to effective, appropriate communication.

Curiously, the word "empathy" itself is relatively new, dating from 1850, but with increased international contacts it's no surprise we're being flooded with books like *The Empathy Gap, Teaching Empathy, Empathy in a Global World* and *The Empathic Civilization*. They represent a seismic shift in how we view the world.

Some neuroscientists now theorize that the human brain possesses neurons, which allow us to feel what is taking place in other people's heads and trigger empathetic comprehension.

But empathy is by no means a new concept brought upon by globalization. The Roman philosopher Cicero (106–43 B.C.) warned, "the whole foundation of human community is threatened by treating foreigners worse than fellow Romans". And, in the 18th century, Immanuel Kant wrote, that "respect for dignity is owed to all humans regardless of their standing in the community." His Scottish contemporary David Hume developed the idea of concentric circles of empathy, meaning people are loyal to their family first, then their village, region and nation in diminishing degrees. But as the world has continued to evolve, the concept has been turned on its head.

Given our multi-media, global-consumption lifestyle — satellite TV, smartphones, Facebook, Twitter, YouTube — we find ourselves increasingly identifying with people in the outermost circles. Virtually everyone on the planet quickly learned of the death of Princess Diana in a car accident in Paris. When Elton John sang *Candle in the Wind* at her funeral, hundreds of millions of people around the world simultaneously shared a personal sense of profound sadness.

But does empathy give you sounder morals or make you more compassionate in intercultural relations? While being empathetic makes people more sensitive to the problems and perspectives of others, it's not clear whether it actually motivates us to take more ethical action. In fact, morality is a culturally-conditioned response.

Various researchers have investigated the connection between empathy and moral action, finding it to be weak at best. City University of New York philosopher Jesse Prinz summed things up in a recent paper: "These studies suggest that empathy is not a major player when it comes to moral motivation. Its contribution is negligible in children, modest in adults, and non-existent when costs are significant." Others term empathy a "fragile flower," easily destroyed by self-interest.

Research found that feelings, such as a short spurt of joy, generate a stronger influence on human actions than empathy. In a famous experiment carried out in the 1970s, researchers placed a 10-cent coin in a phone booth. An amazing 87 % of those who found the dime offered to help a person who accidently dropped some papers nearby a few seconds later. Of the people who didn't find the dime, only 4 % offered to help.

Empathy can be seen more as an intellectual action. As Milton Bennett writes, "it's the ability to recognize and shift context, a core competence of critical thinking." But if there's a personal cost, the process usually stops. You feel sorry for the homeless woman across the street but it's unlikely you're going to cross that street to give her a Euro.

In the internationally acclaimed *Special Flight* undocumented immigrants are filmed in a detention center in Geneva. Viewers sense that Swiss prison officials are struggling to reconcile humane values with the harsh reality of deportation. When the immigrants are handcuffed before being led onto the plane to take them back to their home country, the guards are visibly affected and try to show human solidarity with soothing words — "Don't worry, it's going to turn out all right". Everyone knows it's not true but everyone also knows there's nothing anyone can do. This modicum of kindness, of respect, does both groups good. One border away, the world was horrified when some 300 African refugees drowned trying to reach Lampedusa. The Italian government ordered its navy to save "boat people" in the future but, when other E.U. nations were asked to share in the cost, the response was no.

Prinz points out that empathy also has dark sides. You're likely to care more about cute malnutrition victims than ugly ones. You're more likely to hire someone you know than an anonymous candidate even if the latter is far more qualified. You react to shocking events like hurricanes but are somehow able to ignore the rising CO_2 emissions and global warming that cause them.

What Prinz and others are arguing is that empathy has become a catchword, an emotional shortcut to experience moral solidarity without actual "human" feelings. To put it in another way, it's to share in the illusion of ethical progress — political correctness — without having actually to do something, i.e. to do the dirty work of getting emotionally involved, making judgments and decisions. We're teaching people to cognitively sympathize while doing nothing to help them. Everybody is for empathy, but it isn't enough.

The real movers, those who truly want to change their objective reality and make the world a better place, follow their emotions: anger, disgust, guilt, admiration. These feelings, shaped through cultural conditioning, provide the sentimental groundwork for morality, which translates into values and "sacred" codes. The codes that compel people to perform pro-social actions at whatever cost.

They are often the people the world admires most, such as Albert Schweitzer, awarded the Nobel Peace Prize in 1952 for his years of selfless work with lepers in Gabon. There's no doubt that he had empathic feelings, consciously shifting into their world and generating a sense of common humanity. And this sensation of commonality enabled him to perceive the world in a different way.

"A man is truly ethical only when he obeys the compulsion to help all life which he is able to assist, and shrinks from injuring anything that lives." (Albert Schweitzer)

Empathy told him a leper was feeling pain, isolated, lonely, and this feeling for the other spiked primal anger and disgust that obligated him to seek an alternative action. His ensuing reaction and involvement were based on his sense of obligation to the social, religious and philosophical "certainties" he developed through cultural conditioning. These cultural codes made him react to other people's suffering, not just sympathize.

International hostilities can be understood according to sense of duty. What the conflicts in Ukraine, Russia, Israel and Gaza all have in common is that they're fighting for their existence, for the cultural codes so fundamentally important to them. Debate over which side is morally right is impossible when propaganda takes the place of communication.

The point is that these codes aren't just a set of rules but the basis of one's identity. They reflect passion and joy, material and psychological comfort, ethnocentric emotions and personal commitments. Empathy is just a beginning point, a means to understand the behavior of others.

Interculturalists who hope to improve on the existing world need to help people understand, admire then debate, modify certain beliefs and put their feelings and slightly re-thought codes into action. Invariably there will be conflicts but it's only then we become professionally relevant.

BOOK REVIEWS
AND COMMENTARIES

Book reviews and commentaries

More than thirty years ago there were hardly any publications on intercultural communication. Today, if you look up "intercultural communication" at amazon.com, you will find over 8 300 titles! For the newcomer, it can seem overwhelming. The following reviews are what I personally found to be highly useful for learning and understanding this field.

The last critique deviates from the others as I write about a piece of art, a movie. The film *Das weisse Band* is an impressive statement about the human condition just before World War One, analyzed from an intercultural perspective...

Developing Intercultural Awareness

By Robert Kohls and John Knight,
Intercultural Press (second edition), 143 pages

A lot of people who "might like to become an intercultural facilitator" ask me how I design my workshops and develop the exercises that go along with them. I always come back to the beginning of my career, when I read a how-to book which explains—in clear, step-by-step fashion—the way to put together a solid intercultural course. Even better, it costs less than 20 Euros, maybe the best bargain in our business.

Developing Intercultural Awareness: A Cross-Cultural Training Handbook is drawn from the authors' experience. It contains simulation games, case studies, icebreakers and other activities for developing cross-cultural awareness in virtually any setting. Robert Kohls and John Knight have mapped out one- and two-day workshops for those looking for pre-planned programs, and their appendices include guides to simulation games, films and further reading.

In their second edition, the authors add new and dynamic activities to the array of material already present, ensuring that exercises remain relevant. This easy-to-use guide is both an excellent companion to *The Survival Kit for Overseas Living* and an extremely valuable resource for those looking to train others—or themselves—to become more culturally aware.

A little about Robert Kohls. During the 1950s, he and his wife worked to develop orphanages and schools in Korea. Later, they moved to Washington, where he trained Peace Corps volunteers. He was popular and well-respected, known for his message that intercultural competence is all about compassion and empathy.

Later he became director of training for the U.S. Information Agency and for the Meridian International Center, dedicated to strengthening socio-political understanding. He also helped found SIETAR, which gave him its Primus Inter Pares Award in 1986. With all those credentials, it's no surprise he's the principle author of a timeless gem.

As one intercultural trainer summed it up: "A superb basic guide to cross-cultural training. Kohls and Knight provide an excellent resource to the international trainer seeking general tools or looking toward an expanded repertoire."

International Dimensions of Organizational Behavior

By Nancy J. Adler,
Thompson South Western (fifth edition), 398 pages

Why would we want to review a book that was first published well over 23 years ago? For one simple reason: *International Dimensions of Organizational Behavior* is such a well-written and well-researched work that it has become a standard reference for the majority of intercultural management classes and MBA programs, with over 1 000 000 copies sold. No textbook yet approaches Adler's high standards in explaining how the various dimensions of culture impact global business.

A cursory look shows the extent to which Professor Adler is thorough in her handling of international give-and-take. National culture, workplace behavior and communication differences across cultures, multicultural teamwork and negotiation, synergy and global leadership, the expat experience: all are observed and discussed.

Another reason it's become a classic is Adler's extensive use of vignettes, whether small stories or case studies to explain conceptual and theoretical points. They're lively, direct and above all, perceptive. And the summary and questions-for-reflection at the end of each chapter reinforce and deepen the whole.

In the newly-updated 5th edition, she cites new sources and better case studies, and the writing is even more fluid and concise. The book itself, however, hardly needed to be modified—a testimony to the solid research she put into it back in 1986.

I've used this in my classes for several years and all my students enjoy it. Also when sophisticated business people ask me what I recommend to avoid intercultural mishaps, I refer them to Nancy Adler. If you familiarize yourself with all the points she makes, you won't need anything else. She's put everything you need to know about living and working across cultures into one compact volume.

Basic Concepts of Intercultural Communications—
Paradigms, Principles and Practices

By Milton J. Bennett
Intercultural Press (second edition), 334 pages

In his new book, *Basic Concepts of Intercultural Communications,* Milton Bennett sets himself the ambitious goal of conveying the essence of intercultural theory. It is a thought-provoking compendium of 13 texts, providing a concise and coherent overview. Bennett's profound love for intercultural issues comes through clearly in this updated second edition. Six chapters are from his own writings and the others are from time-tested classics that every interculturalist should know.

As with the first edition 15 years ago, he dissects intercultural communication from the early days of relativism to the constructivist nature of the field today. What's different are the first five chapters, major additions that take into account today's fast-evolving

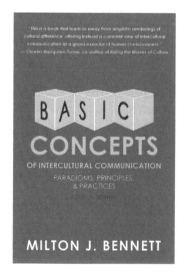

multicultural societies and reconcile the basic principles of intercultural communication with current applications in education and business.

Like his *DMIS model*, he sequences the texts in terms of complexity, ensuring that the reader progressively attains the level of competent understanding. What I enjoyed most was Bennett's first chapter, *A Constructivist Frame for Intercultural Communication*. Drawing from the theories of Kelly, Brown and von Foerster, he writes that we don't perceive events directly; our experiences are, instead, built through templates, a set of categories with which we organize our perception.

Striving to fully understand the constructivist approach, I read this chapter again and again. All the while, as constructivist theory states, my mind was constructing new templates which I then used to arrange and widen my awareness. Or, to put it in another way, I became increasingly sensitive to the constructive explanation of intercultural relationships. I couldn't help but feel the very real joy of learning, the "ecstasy" of finally comprehending!

Bennett distinctly points out that obtaining intellectual understanding is not in an end in itself; its purpose is to generate an alternative experience, that of becoming sensitive to the feeling of appropriateness that accompanies a new template. This intuitive grasp provides a deeper intercultural experience for trainers, who can then facilitate others in acquiring their own experiences.

Without condescension or false complexity, he concludes the chapter eloquently. "Then, and only then, can we truly consider ourselves capable of exercising and teaching intercultural competence."

In his second chapter, *Intercultural Epistemology and Paradigmatic Confusion,* he develops his leitmotiv, "coherent theory generates powerful practice". This is where Bennett's intellectual brilliance shines, as he systematically describes the epistemological assumptions of the positivist, relativist and constructivist paradigms, and what their implications mean for intercultural theory.

Briefly, the positivist treats culture as having a static existence, which can be observed objectively. The relativist thinks of culture as a closed system with a set of roles and rules used as a frame of reference in understanding other cultures. And the constructivist sees culture as built on social foundations necessitating a dialectic "other perspective".

A stickler for coherent, logical analysis, Bennett points out that if the paradigm underlying a practice is different than that of the claimed outcome, the resulting incoherence weakens the practice and harms the overall credibility of the field. Bennett makes his point with the popular iceberg metaphor many practitioners use to describe culture.

Although the vast majority of intercultural facilitators understand culture as a dynamic process, generating artifacts and patterns of behavior, many still insist on comparing culture to the static iceberg, a positivist notion. Students are told that what we see is the tip of the iceberg. Ninety percent of the culture lies beneath the surface, where invisible assumptions and values are waiting to surprise and trap the unsuspecting foreign sojourner.

It's a clever comparison and provokes lively images of a Titanic-like disaster but it's essentially transmitting the wrong message. One comes away with the idea that culture is a "thing", a stationary object. Yet if one accepts the constructivist approach, that culture is a dialectic process, coordinating meanings and actions, then the positivist iceberg contradicts the inherently complex nature of culture.

Other parts of the book add new perspectives, such as *Stumbling Blocks in Intercultural Communication,* an excellent primer on the ins and outs of intercultural education by LaRay M. Barna. Taking a constructivist perspective, the author sees "assumption of similarity" as the most difficult obstacle to overcome when people of different backgrounds interact. Effective intercultural relations come from the ability to see and construe relevant cultural differences.

What struck throughout was Bennett's overwhelming desire to provide selective writings, which build a coherent framework. *Basic Concepts of Intercultural Communication* is an exacting work that challenges our thoughts and inclinations. Illuminating the subject in unexpected ways, it develops the mind and serves to provide a new view of things through renovated eyes.

Milton Bennett is an educator (from the Latin *educatio:* to bring up). A groomer of talent, one who has the gift to impart a deeper understanding of things and supplies the tools with which to increase that understanding. Explaining without being heavy-handed, exposing without imposing, his work brings the mind to full flower and offers readers fulfillment they might not find otherwise. The book is demanding but, at the same time, of lasting substance. An outstanding achievement.

Intercultural Interaction — A Multidisciplinary Approach to Intercultural Communication

By Helen Spencer-Oatey and Peter Franklin
Palgrave MacMillan, 367 pages

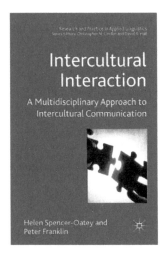

Whether you're a professor, a researcher or a student who wants to know about current ideas and practices in intercultural relations (or interaction — the preferred term of the authors), this is the book for you. Simply put, it delivers an excellent survey of all on-going discussions and research in the intercultural field.

The authors Spencer-Oatey and Franklin carefully define their title in the introduction. "Intercultural" refers to cultural distance between people when significant enough to have an effect on communication that is noticeable to at least one of the parties. "Interaction" emphasizes the activity of people communicating to each other, which is very different from the usual (static) studies in which the language and/or behavior of two groups is compared. Furthermore, it draws attention to the dynamic and dialectic nature of language and behavior.

Although this distinction might appear as nitpicking to the reader, the authors firmly believe it provides the groundwork for a clearer understanding of "cultural behavior" and "idiosyncratic behaviour". Their analysis will help people manage cross-cultural encounters more effectively.

The book is divided into four parts, beginning with the conceptual issues of culture and the adaptation and impact of language and culture on understanding (defined as intercultural interaction competence). Part Two explores instruments for measuring and assessing intercultural interactional competence as well its development. The third section focuses on research: topics that can be investigated and the methods for doing so. Finally, the authors offer a solid list of resources for further study.

I found chapter nine, *Development Competence in Intercultural Interaction* (pages 199–241), especially informative — a fine summary of the methods necessary for intercultural development in both the professional and academic worlds. Classical transfer of knowledge, even in the classroom, isn't sufficient; developing skills and changing attitudes is also necessary.

The authors go on to classify methods and their expected results. A lecture or briefing brings about a "knowledge outcome", for example, while a critical incident develops knowledge, skills and attitudes. For trainers like myself, it's a lucid overview for assessing the needs of workshop participants.

This book is a state-of-the-art encyclopedia of intercultural research. At the same time, extensive use of stories and case studies makes abstract conceptual and theoretical points more lively, more direct. It's a work that's sure to inspire further investigation by students and scholars.

Empathy in the Global World — An Intercultural Perspective

By Carolyn Calloway-Thomas
Sage Publications, 250 pages

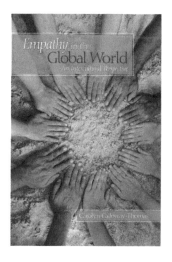

As any good trainer knows, empathy is deeply embedded in, and inseparable from, intercultural sensitivity. And it's no surprise that an increasing number of books on the subject have been published in recent years. But *Empathy in the Global World* goes beyond the usual examination of "the cultural other" by touching on geopolitics, class issues, international NGOs and national disasters. Simply put, it's an excellent distillation of the historical, political and psychological aspects of empathy.

The first two chapters provide some fascinating background. We learn, for instance, that the Roman philosopher Cicero (106 – 43 B.C.) warned "the whole foundation of the human community is threatened by treating foreigners worse than fellow Romans." And Immanuel Kant noted in the 18th century that "respect for dignity is owed to all humans regardless of their standing in the community."

His Scottish contemporary David Hume developed the idea of concentric circles of empathy, meaning people are loyal to their family first, then their village, region and nation in diminishing degrees. But as the world has continued to evolve, the concept has been turned on its head.

Given our modern, media-consumption lifestyle, we often find ourselves identifying with people in the outermost circles. Virtually everyone on the planet with access to television or the Internet was horrified as the twin towers of the World Trade Center cast up their columns of smoke on Sept 11th, 2001. When they finally collapsed, horror was transformed into a sense of profound sadness—somehow personally felt—among hundreds of millions of people around the world.

Conversely, as Chapter 4 points out, globalization is changing our attitudes toward empathy in another way. The shock of 9/11 and subsequent train and subway bombings in Madrid and London have led—as terrorism is wont to do—to a pervasive atmosphere of suspicion and fear of "the cultural other". Additionally, massive immigration coupled with high birth-rates among minority cultures has generated permanent demographic changes in both North America and Western Europe. Calloway-Thomas points out that when numerical balance poses a threat to indigenous society, empathy takes a back seat to national identity.

All this provides the groundwork for her concluding chapters on how we, as global citizens, can develop knowledge and information-based skills—or empathetic literacy— to better respond to cross-cultural encounters. *Ten Basic Rules of Intercultural Relations* is an excellent summary and can be used in any workshop.

All in all, the work is a goldmine of information for students, professors, trainers and even politicians searching for new ways to understand and address human problems on a global scale.

Developing Intercultural Competence and Transformation —
Theory, Research, and Application in International Education

Edited by Victor Savicki
Stylus Publishing, 375 pages

As international education programs become more and more popular (and more and more necessary), those who construct and conduct them have to do their homework. The field is rapidly evolving, new ideas every day; how to marry them with the tried-and-true?

How to take the best of a myriad of methods, approaches, exercises and form your own unique forum? Intercultural competence is about personal growth and that of the teacher is what maximizes that of his or her students.

Dr. Savicki has done a wonderful job of synthesis here. His book provides not only ideas for curriculum, but also the theory and research which back them up. Compiling the experiences of no less than 17 top international educators, he divides their work into three sections: theories for intercultural growth and transformation, research, and applications. Savicki's goal, as his editor puts it, "is to help international educators create study-abroad experiences that reach their goals by design, not chance."

Among other things, international educators have to understand "intercultural competence" and "transformation" as non-tangible processes, which will always remain elusive in terms of grading. The thread emerges that cross-cultural fluency is based on the development of subtle, almost intuitive skills. Difficult to measure, sometimes frustrating to teach, they are also incredibly rewarding once mastered.

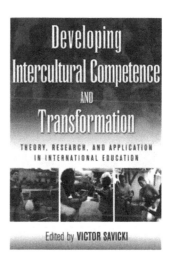

Perhaps the most basic ability is to "objectively" — or, as I like to say, non-subjectively — observe and interpret one's own day-to-day experiences. Facilitators agree that students who keep a *DIE journal* (describe, interpret, evaluate) greatly accelerate their appreciation of the extent to which reality differs according to the eyes and ears of the perceiver.

Another important point: students need to be guided on how to work through culture shock. If not, and without even realizing what's happening to them, they risk being overwhelmed. The teacher, as both counselor and confidant, must focus on their emotional state so as to slowly transform confusion and anxiety into intellectual demystification and empathetic comprehension.

Closely related is the sharing of experiences among students, often an amusing collection of misconceptions. (In-group/out-group distinctions can be made to encourage a wider perspective and ease the way for frame shifting.) In the end, an educator promotes strong attention to self-reflection.

Dr. Savicki's case studies, narratives, and class techniques lay the foundation for a solid international-education program in the *Age of Obama*. And the book has the added benefit of coming out just when there are more and more teachers—not to mention students—who can definitely use it...

Third Culture Kids — Growing Up Among Worlds

By David C. Pollock and Ruth E. Van Reken
Nicholas Brealey Publishing, 306 pages

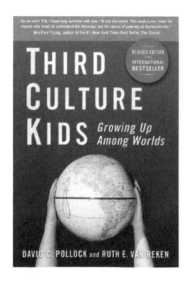

We continuously talk about the necessity of developing intercultural competence, defined as the ability to adapt and communicate appropriately and effectively in a large variety of socio-ethnic settings. For the majority of us, it's a mind-set that doesn't come naturally.

People need to spend time abroad learning to gradually generate cognitive brain shifting and a new repertoire of behaviors. Yet, there's a group of people who seem to naturally possess this tool.

Authors Ruth van Reken and David Pollock were the first to report in 1999 on the phenomenon with their book *Third Culture Kids*. In their revised, more complete 2009 edition, they expand on the growing complexity of the term. TCK usually refers to the children of expatriate, military or diplomatic families, but now the authors introduce a new category: cross-cultural kids, who are international adoptees or children of biracial or bicultural parents.

The increasing number of such culturally mixed offspring is the future, the "new normal" in our globalized world and Barack Obama is the paramount example. Not only is he a true African-American (with close relatives on both continents), he spent part of his childhood in Asia as the "stepson" of an Indonesian Muslim.

The authors offer a simple definition of the TCK/CCK profile—children (up to age 18) who spend a significant period of their developmental years in a culture outside their parents' "passport country". Somewhat like their parents, but in a far more extreme immersion, they have a sense of simultaneously belonging to the host and "home" societies without any real ownership of either. Elements from both (or multiple) cultures are blended, resulting in a unique individual.

And what are the traits that make them so different from the norm? To begin with, they possess an inherent capacity for objective observation coupled with cross-cultural skills such as flexibility and tolerance. They respect differences and are willing to learn from them; they never assume that their way of doing things is best.

Their worldview allows them to experience true diversity and develop an acceptance of people for who they are, regardless of race or nationality. And they're quick to think outside the box, appreciating and reconciling different habits and beliefs.

Of course, there's also a downside. TCKs and CCKs often talk about varying degrees of rootlessness, a sense of being profoundly connected to people and places around the world yet somehow cut off from them as well. Frequent, painful good-byes leave them unable to bond with others or identify with any one culture, leading to a breakdown of identity. To cope, they learn to exist on the periphery. The idea of commitment or intimacy is accompanied by tremendous insecurity.

The end result is restlessness, the need to always be on the move. Ironically, if they form strong relationships, it's usually with those who share their sense of rootlessness—other TCKs and CCKs. Not surprisingly, they are multilingual, extremely open toward others and have an innate capacity for cultural frame-shifting. In their subjective worldview, however, they feel a strange, floating sense of non-identity. They may sound French, American and German in turn but they are none of these… and all of them too.

The greatest challenge for maturing TCK/CCK is to forge a sense of personal identity from the various environments to which they've been exposed. By addressing difficult experiences, they win the possibility of exploiting their intercultural knowledge and talents.

Pollock and van Reken give good advice on how to put the past into context and be all the stronger for it. The contradictory aspects of being a TCK/CCK are explored and, ultimately, celebrated. The book is well written, with numerous interviews and anecdotes which make the concepts easy to grasp.

At times, the authors seem to repeat points—the challenges and benefits in Part II seem somewhat overdone—but this is a relatively minor point. *Third Culture Kids* is definitely the reference on coming of age in a multicultural setting.

It's a must-read for anyone who wishes to understand how traditional notions of identity and "home" are being radically changed by the ceaseless patterns of global mobility. And perhaps especially those who feel threatened by social evolution. For in the end, despite some very real challenges, it's a wonderful gift indeed to grow up spanning two or more worlds.

Cultures and Organizations — Software of the Mind

By Geert Hofstede, Gert J. Hofstede, and Michael Minkov
McGraw Hill (third edition), 561 pages

Perhaps no other social scientist in the last 30 years has revolutionized the field of culture and business more than Geert Hofstede. Because his initial book *Cultural Consequences* was considered to be too "scientific" for most people, he published a simpler and more accessible version—*Cultures and Organizations*—in 1991. This version became an instant best-seller, translated into 18 languages.

This revised, third edition (2010) offers a monumental perspective on cultural and organizational paradigms. The first section begins with an excellent overview of culture and explains the concept of "dimension"—an aspect of culture that can be measured relative to other cultures. The three authors then examine nations according to a six-dimensional plan and the culture of organizations. The final section deals with the implications of cultural differences.

The work itself features substantial additions and new contributions. Among other things, Michael Minkov reveals a novel, sixth cultural dimension: indulgence versus restraint. The gratification of basic desires, such as happiness, leisure and life-control, is juxtaposed with our very human guilt at "wasting" time or money. The statistical results explain why Filipinos, for example, are far more content than the citizens of Hong Kong.

Another absorbing chapter relates the 2002 study asking 1800 MBA students in 17 different countries what they considered the priorities of business to be. Americans listed growth, respect for ethical norms, personal wealth, this year's profits and power. Quite a contrast with the German "top five" of social responsibility, respect for employees, innovation, profits ten years from now and ethical norms. These types of differences allow us to better understand national character and idiomatic behavior... such as why the 2008 sub-prime loan crisis was born in the USA.

The final chapter—written by Geert's son Gert—gives a Darwinian spin to the evolution of societies and shows why we shouldn't expect global monoculturalism any time soon. And *vive la différence!*

BOOK REVIEWS AND COMMENTARIES

Easy-to-understand tables summarize key concepts throughout, as do a plethora of entertaining anecdotes. I found myself returning to the multidimensional index scores as I pondered those differences. And then plunging on to read more.

The writing is fluid and helps us along but it must be noted that this is a very long book—a bit too long. Nonetheless, it's a reader-friendly introduction to cross-cultural research and a definite "must" for anyone trying to understand our turbulent new century.

American Ways — A Cultural Guide to the United States

By Gary Althen with Janet Bennett
Intercultural Press, 279 pages

Understanding one's own culture is challenging enough; trying to explain it to others leaves most people at a loss for words. We don't usually give much thought to our up-bringing and the tendency is to treat it in an uncritical light. To provide a balanced view, both positive and negative characteristics must be presented. But accepting one's culture "warts and all" is difficult.

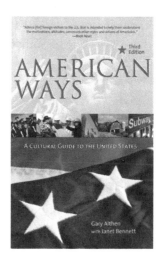

And it's only the first step; the second is even harder. When pointing out unfavorable aspects of our "people", we can't help but feel we're betraying family, tribe, nation. The best descriptions of culture usually come from the outside. Alexis de Tocqueville's *Democracy in America* is just one example but his observations still ring true 180 years later—despite upheavals in the outside world, individual societies change incrementally.

Still, a few people are able to portray their own culture astutely enough to distinguish themselves in the cross-cultural equation. Gary Althen and Janet Bennett are in this category and their *American Ways* captures the American spirit in all its facets.

Althen wrote the first (1988) and second (2003) editions but this third one (2010) has been updated, and enriched, with the help of Janet Bennett. Insightful and honest, the authors succeed in making American culture understandable to foreigners and compatriots alike. The language is clear and examples abound to illustrate their conclusions.

Organized into 23 chapters, the book delves into customs, values, styles of communication, patterns of thinking and national behavior in general. The first part deals with concepts such as individualism, freedom and competitiveness, providing fodder for class discussions and a solid basis for intercultural awareness. Part two part explores everyday American life: politics, media, education and relationships. Presented in matter-of-fact narration, each chapter offers concrete suggestions for foreigners living in, or visiting, the U.S. The last section, on coping with differences, examines classic themes like culture shock and the benefits of keeping a journal.

What I liked most was a look at communication styles which surprised me with insights into my own background. The authors point out that Americans are masters of "small talk" as a way to avoid class-oriented intellectualism; we don't get much practice in debating ideas but—unlike what many non-Americans think—it doesn't mean we're incapable of serious reflection and analysis.

At the same time, Americans love it when their media paint contemporary issues as black-and-white struggles. And political leaders have long ceased to search for common ground: virtually every word is an attack in an never-ending ideological war. The public is always entertained but seldom educated.

American Ways is based in solid research and delivers original variations on a well-known theme. It's must-reading for almost anybody interested in the country, including those who were born there.

Managing Cross-Cultural Communication — Principles & Practice

By Barry Maude
Palgrave Macmillan, 369 pages

This is the type of book I wish I had had when I was beginning my work as a trainer and consultant. It's an exceptionally well-researched and comprehensive review of all we need to know about intercultural communication. And done in a serious and readable manner.

As the subtitle suggests, the book comes in two parts—principles and practices. Maude begins by examining the concept of culture as a logical starting point for understanding the process of cross-cultural communication and then skillfully denotes how values are a major source of difference in attitudes and behaviors. In the 3rd chapter, he provides proof on how language strongly impacts our perception, coupled with a discussion on how English dominates the global flow of information. In chapter five, the author deconstructs prejudice and stereotyping—presenting a very good overview of these two closely related concepts.

The second part is what I found most useful—the practical application of theory to practice. In seven chapters, Maude covers the nuts and bolts of our profession: expatriate performance, the development of cross-cultural skills, communicating across cultural distance, managing and working in multicultural teams, cross-cultural meetings and negotiations as well as interviews and selection. His texts are backed up with summaries of research findings, small exercises, mini-case studies, examples and personal anecdotes. The reader can only come away with a feeling of being given an exhaustive and thorough review of all the issues of globalized communication. In fact, each topic is so well investigated that a clever consultant just starting in the profession can extract the information and offer practical (if not remarkable) solutions to a client's intercultural problem.

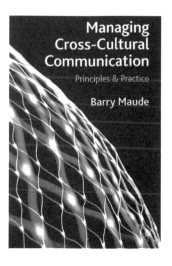

My favorite chapter was the one on developing cross-cultural skills. The author here provides new, refreshing ideas on basic rules of training. As he notes, research shows overwhelmingly that the most effective way to provide cross-cultural skills is through interactive work. It only reconfirms what I've observed in my own trainings: participants best absorb knowledge through game simulations (often fun and silly), resulting in effective changes in cognitive behavior. Another point he makes is that one-to-one coaching may be an expensive way of developing cross-cultural skills, but is extremely effective, provided that the facilitator is capable and well informed.

One element of criticism—the layout is, sad to say, dull and uninspiring. In this day and age of multi-media visualization, the publisher could have put more resources into graphic design, creating a book that would have literally "communicated" to its readers. Nonetheless, the content is second to none—informative, perceptive and engaging. Maude breaks down the vast range of knowledge and literature to give a broad and practical view of what intercultural communications is all about. A must-have reference book for any trainer or consultant in the field.

The movie "Das weisse Band" (The White Ribbon)

Directed by Michael Haneke
Germany/Austria/France/Italy 2009, 144 minutes

Acclaimed worldwide and winning many awards, including the *Palme d'Or* in Cannes in 2009, *Das weisse Band* is a one of those rare, powerful films that absorbs you completely as it examines the real nature of being human.

Shot in stunning black and white, it's a story of a series of mysterious events in a German village just before the outbreak of World War I. Done with superb editing, acute attention to pre-1914 detail, clinically frank dialogue and first-class acting, its explores with frightful brilliance the many facets of evil: vengeance, feudalism, rigid hierarchies, religious intolerance, sexual repression, violence, child abuse.

There're scenes of the overly strict Pastor, who subjects his own children to cruel punishment, aimed at enforcing unthinking obedience. The patriarchal baron's eldest son goes missing on the day of the harvest festival and is found the following morning, bound and whipped with a cane. The doctor treats the village children kindly, but at night, shames and humiliates his housekeeper by means of cruel verbal assaults and sexually abuses his 14-year old daughter. It's a stunning, thought-provoking work that will polarize audiences.

Although producer Michael Haneke uses a German cultural backdrop for his parable, these acts of evil could happen in any country. It's a cautionary tale that suggests that the roots of war and hatred lie not in ideology, but in the corruption of our values and the emptiness in our souls.

Curiously though, none of the critical reviews have touched on the historical and cultural aspect of this film. It's not only a masterful study of the *Kaiser Wilhelm II* epoch, but in some indirect way provides clues to Germany's ways and norms of today. Granted, Germany of 2013 doesn't at all resemble the old authoritarian order of 1914. Since the debacle of World War II, traditional values of order, duty and discipline have been examined, questioned, debated and their extreme aspects have been abandoned.

Yet, the German soul and its core values date from century-old roots; they are still there, cherished in the heart, whether it be in Berlin, Düsseldorf or Stuttgart. The adage "cultures don't change" is reaffirmed clearly in this film. However, the film struck me in a much more profound way. Upon watching the scenes, it reminded me of my own experiences as an 11-year old American boy in the Alsatian village of my grandparents. Although officially part of France, the village fifty years ago was still very much German with its Alsatian dialect and semi-authoritarian and patriarchal-like structures. At first, I didn't understand this new and strange culture. But it was only upon returning to Los Angeles after 15 months in this Alsatian village, that this reality became a part of me.

And this is why I found *Das weisse Band* so revealing and rewarding—it provoked a rediscovery of a world that had long left me, but still is affecting my outlook and perception of life.

Index

About the author

PATRICK SCHMIDT has been active in the field of intercultural communication for over 25 years. American by birth and education, he left the U.S. soon after finishing his studies and spent the next three decades living and working in France, Germany, Austria, Canada and Malaysia. His years of association with the German automobile industry led to his first book *Understanding American and German Business Cultures*. His second book, *In Search of Intercultural Understanding,* is a practical guide to cross-cultural survival. He has served as president of SIETAR Europa and is presently editor-in-chief of the *SIETAR Europa Journal*. He lives in Strasbourg, France.

Lightning Source UK Ltd.
Milton Keynes UK
UKOW06f1114251114

242140UK00006B/51/P